APPROVED

APPROVED

How to Get Your
BUSINESS LOAN
Funded Faster, Cheaper
& with Less Stress

PHIL WINN

New York

APPROVED

How to Get Your **BUSINESS LOAN** Funded Faster, Cheaper & with Less Stress

Published in New York, New York, by Morgan James Publishing. Morgan James and The Entrepreneurial Publisher are trademarks of Morgan James, LLC.
www.MorganJamesPublishing.com

The Morgan James Speakers Group can bring authors to your live event. For more information or to book an event visit The Morgan James Speakers Group at www.TheMorganJamesSpeakersGroup.com.

A **free** eBook edition is available with the purchase of this print book.

CLEARLY PRINT YOUR NAME ABOVE IN UPPER CASE

Instructions to claim your free eBook edition:
1. Download the BitLit app for Android or iOS
2. Write your name in **UPPER CASE** on the line
3. Use the BitLit app to submit a photo
4. Download your eBook to any device

ISBN 978-1-63047-563-5 paperback
ISBN 978-1-63047-564-2 eBook
Library of Congress Control Number:
2015901930

Cover Design by:
Rachel Lopez
www.r2cdesign.com

Interior Design by:
Bonnie Bushman
bonnie@caboodlegraphics.com

In an effort to support local communities and raise awareness and funds, Morgan James Publishing donates a percentage of all book sales for the life of each book to Habitat for Humanity Peninsula and Greater Williamsburg.

Get involved today, visit
www.MorganJamesBuilds.com

Habitat
for Humanity®
Peninsula and
Greater Williamsburg
Building Partner

For my son, Kaydin Jackson Winn

TABLE OF CONTENTS

INTRODUCTION

Congratulations on making this important step toward business loan approval.

Applying for a business loan can be difficult, time intensive, and expensive, but it doesn't have to be. This book was written to provide a straightforward road map to help you obtain approval.

In Part One, traditional business loans are compared to business loans backed by the Small Business Administration (SBA) based on 21 factors. In these first two chapters, you will learn why every entrepreneur should consider an SBA loan.

In Part Two, an overview of the SBA's flagship programs is discussed, including how to meet the SBA's eligibility requirements, a low bar if you follow the guidelines in this book.

In Part Three, you will learn how to evaluate yourself, your partners, and your business(es) from a lender's perspective. With this knowledge, you will be able to highlight particular strengths that lenders want to see and mitigate weaknesses that could cause processing delays and even loan declination.

In Part Four, you will learn how to prepare a summary business plan specifically written to obtain financing. A business plan is necessary for financing to take advantage of growth opportunities, acquisition of third-party businesses, and new businesses. In Part Four, you will learn which parts of the business plan to devote more time to and which other sections only need limited information or may be skipped altogether.

In Part Five, you will learn how to prepare your business loan application correctly. Incomplete/incorrect applications cause major delays in the loan approval process. Practically speaking, complete applications always take priority over the incomplete ones. Incomplete applications are often just set aside regardless of when they were initially submitted. In fact, many lenders will simply decline them due to the time that it takes to educate borrowers on how to properly prepare a complete application.

After finishing this book, you will have the ability to highlight the strengths (and mitigate the weaknesses) of your business from a lender's perspective, provide a simple business plan identifying how your business will be profitable for the long term, and accurately prepare a business loan application package that can be immediately submitted through underwriting without delay.

As of fiscal year ending September 30, 2014, the US Small Business Administration enabled small businesses to obtain more than $23 billion in business funding. For fiscal year 2015, the SBA has budgeted to support more than $32 billion in business funding.

This is your year to obtain financing to transition your business to the next level.

PART ONE
21 REASONS WHY YOU WANT AN SBA LOAN

When evaluating various types of business financing, it is important to understand your options. Too often, decisions are made about products and services before evaluating the short- and long-term benefits and weaknesses. For any big financial decision, such as applying for a business loan, it is important to understand how the loan will impact you and your business at the time of application through the day that you make your last payment. In chapters one and two, you will get a thorough understanding of the pros and cons of conventional lending as compared to SBA lending. Be prepared to be surprised.

If you want to get a loan for your business, an SBA loan should be your number one choice. In chapters one and two, conventional and SBA business loan programs will be compared based on 21 categories. The 21 categories to be discussed are:

1. *Collateral*
2. *Cash Flow*
3. *Eligibility*
4. *Loan to Value*
5. *Down Payment*

Are you ready? Let's get started.

CHAPTER 1

WHY YOU WANT AN SBA LOAN: REASONS 1-11

1) <u>Collateral</u>

Collateral will be evaluated at the onset of a lender receiving an application. Collateral is really important to lenders because if a business fails, it is their first and sometimes only option to try to get their money back. The result of the collateral analysis will impact your conventional and SBA loan approval differently.

Collateral—Conventional Commercial Financing

Conventional commercial loans must meet two initial requirements at the time of application. The number one requirement is that the loan is supported by historical cash flow. The number two requirement is that the loan is fully secured by collateral. For a new business, a business looking to expand, a business that leases its space, and for several other scenarios, lack of adequate collateral is one of the top reasons why most loans are declined for conventional commercial financing. If your business owns and occupies the commercial real estate that you are looking to finance, you are likely to only be able to obtain financing for up to 80% of the value of the real estate. If you are applying for a loan to purchase commercial real estate for your business, you are likely to get loan approval for the lower of 80% of the purchase price or 80% of the appraised value of the property.

Collateral—SBA Financing

While all available collateral is generally required by the SBA to fully secure the loan, there are many circumstances in which there isn't enough collateral available to do so. Under the SBA's primary loan program, the SBA 7(a) loan program, loans can actually be obtained for up to $5 million without any collateral. For example, if you want to purchase a business that is for sale for $6 million and absolutely no collateral is available, you can qualify for SBA financing for up to $5 million if the business cash flow and other noncollateral factors support the transaction. As to be discussed in the loan term section, this unsecured $5 million loan can also be repaid over 10 years or longer. Obtaining this type of financing through conventional means without the SBA is highly unlikely.

2) Cash Flow

Cash flow is one of the first items evaluated upon submission of a loan application. The evaluation of cash flow determines a business's ability to afford debt. Cash flow will be evaluated on a historical and projected basis. The results of the cash flow analysis will impact your conventional and SBA loan approval differently.

Cash Flow—Conventional Commercial Financing

For conventional loans, it is much easier to obtain financing for companies with proven cash flow histories. For example, if you are applying for a loan and the payment is $5,000 per month or $60,000 per year, the bank will want to see on your tax returns and financial statements for at least the last two years that at least $60,000 is available after all expenses and all other debt payments have been paid. Banks actually want to see that your business can afford 125% of the proposed new debt amount but we'll get into this later on in the book.

The point is that if you are a new business (in business less than two years), you will not qualify for traditional commercial bank financing because you will not be able to prove this. If your business has been around for a while and you are looking to expand into a larger facility or purchase additional equipment so that you can generate more sales, the proposed new debt will be added to your existing debt to determine if your business's historical cash flow can support the expansion. This again can be a challenge under traditional commercial financing requirements.

Cash Flow—SBA Financing
Under an SBA loan, your business can qualify for cash flow coverage based on either a historical or a projected cash flow basis. This opens the door to start-up companies, new businesses, existing businesses, businesses needing capital to expand, and more. With sound projections supported by other applicant information, obtaining capital to make your business dreams a reality is within reach through the SBA. The amount of cash flow needed on a historical or a projected basis will be discussed in Part Three. I will also walk you through exactly how to prepare financing projections supported by reasonable assumptions in the business plan chapter (Part Four).

3) <u>Eligibility</u>
Eligibility goes hand in hand with credit quality and risk avoidance. Meeting the requirement of a conventional loan program versus an SBA loan program varies greatly for eligibility.

Eligibility—Conventional Commercial Financing
Strict bank requirements make it difficult for entrepreneurs to qualify for conventional commercial loans. Commercial loans typically must be fully secured, the borrower must have a track record of several years of positive cash flow, guarantors must have good credit scores, low leverage must be demonstrated, and numerous other requirements must be satisfied. Inadequate historical cash flow and the lack of adequate collateral are the two top reasons conventional commercial loans are declined. In addition, a bank may decline

a loan that is fully secured and has good cash flow but is not of an industry that the bank wants to lend to. For example, many banks are unwilling to loan money to restaurants.

Eligibility—SBA Financing

SBA loans on the other hand have a low bar when it comes to eligibility. Historical cash flow is not necessary if projected financial statements support the application request. Full collateral security is not required if it is not available. Almost every type of industry is eligible for financing other than the few listed in Part Two. SBA loan eligibility will be discussed in detail in Part Two. Throughout this book, I will discuss several practical scenarios in which you will have the opportunity to compare SBA and conventional commercial financing eligibility.

4) Loan to Value

Loan to value is the ratio of debt to asset value expressed as a percentage. For instance, if you have a mortgage on your home with a balance of $80,000 and your house is worth $100,000, your loan to value is 80%. The result of the loan-to-value calculation will impact your conventional and SBA loan approval differently.

Loan to Value—Conventional Commercial Financing

When applying for financing at a bank, loans are advanced based on a percentage of value. If you purchase a car, you may get 100% financing. If you purchase a house, getting a first mortgage of 80% loan to value (LTV) is typical. In some cases, you can get a second and even a third mortgage on your home to get to a higher combined LTV. In traditional commercial financing, LTV tends to be lower as businesses have greater risk of failure than car or home loans. Commercial lenders are often reluctant or unwilling to exceed 80% LTV on commercial buildings and equipment. For special purpose properties such as a car wash or gas station, the loan to value can be as low as 50%. Loan to value is determined by each bank and is detailed in their credit policies. Credit policy details the lender's lending policies including their comfort level for LTV based on collateral type. On a commercial real estate purchase, the lender may offer

80% LTV so the borrower will have to come to closing with the 20% down payment plus additional money for closing costs.

Loan to Value—SBA Financing

The SBA programs are designed to promote cash flow lending rather than collateral lending (LTV lending). To encourage cash flow lending, the SBA has actually made it a requirement of SBA lenders to not restrict SBA loans based on high LTV. The rule states that SBA lenders may not decline a loan solely based on a shortfall of collateral. Many SBA loans far exceed traditional LTV requirements and are considered to be highly unsecured. In addition, the SBA requires no equity injection (down payment) on commercial real estate financed when intangible assets are not included. When intangible assets are financed as part of a real estate acquisition, a business valuation may be required to support the intangible value. Again, no equity injection is required if the business valuation supports the SBA loan amount and loan approval is handled through standard SBA processing. Most SBA lenders require at least a 10% injection, which obviously is much better than the 20% or more injection required in conventional financing. The possibility of obtaining business financing in excess of the value of the commercial real estate makes the SBA program extremely competitive for commercial loan options.

5) <u>Down Payment</u>

Down payment, also known as equity injection, is the amount of money that you have to put into a deal for a lender to be comfortable to finance the balance. The amount of down payment required for conventional financing versus SBA financing varies greatly.

Down Payment—Conventional Commercial Financing

Working capital is critical for a business's survival. Without it, businesses have difficulty buying in bulk, covering accounts payable, payroll, operating expenses, repairs and maintenance, taxes, acquiring new equipment, making down payments on real estate, etc. Traditional commercial loans require from 20% to 25% down and sometimes more equity toward the purchase of real estate. Equipment purchases can require much higher down payments. Conventional lenders impose these requirements to make sure that if they have to foreclose and take the property back that they can sell it fairly quickly and cover the outstanding loan balance and their expenses. If the owner's equity interest is too low (i.e., the LTV is too high) because the lender did not require the borrower to personally invest enough money, the bank is likely to lose money in a foreclosure. Coming up with the capital to cover the required injection (down payment) for your project often puts excessive strain on your business and can be a deal breaker. It may also force you to look to outside investment sources to come up with the capital. Outside investment can be a great thing as it enables you to get the capital that you need for the down payment but has the downside of reducing your ownership interest, which can change the dynamics of management.

Down Payment—SBA Financing

The SBA understands the value of working capital. Working capital is needed on a daily basis for most businesses, and the SBA understands that businesses are usually stressed for working capital due to uncollected accounts receivable, swings in cash flow, and other variables. The SBA is much more flexible with its equity injection requirements than conventional lenders. For real estate purchases, the SBA itself actually requires no equity injection; however, most SBA lenders require a 10% down payment. A 10% injection is obviously much more favorable than the 20% to 25% required by conventional commercial lenders. If you are unable to come up with the down payment on your own, raising capital from outside investors of only 10% versus 20% to 25% will enable you to keep much more of the ownership of the company and management control.

6) <u>Term Length</u>

Term length is the amount of time that the lender approves your loan to be repaid. For commercial real estate mortgages, the term is usually a much shorter period of time than the amortization period on which your regular monthly payments are based. The term length can be significantly different between conventional and SBA loan programs.

Term Length—Conventional Commercial Financing

Most commercial loans are offered with repayment terms that are either too short, based on the useful life of the asset on which the financing is based, or too short because of maturities that put unnecessary stress on a business's cash flow. For example, it is common for equipment that is intended to be used by a business for 15 years to be financed over a five- to seven-year period with conventional commercial financing. It is also common for commercial real estate to be financed based on a 20- to 25-year amortization but only with a five-year term. The five-year term is way too short to repay the entire loan balance, so the business is forced to refinance or requalify to extend the term. Continually having to requalify every five years puts a lot of stress on business owners. Applying for financing can seem like a full-time job in itself, so trying to run a productive business and apply for financing can impair productivity.

Term Length—SBA Financing

SBA loans typically have longer terms than their traditional commercial counterparts. Unlike the conventional commercial real estate loan with a 20-year amortization and a 5-year term, the SBA real estate loan will have a 25-year amortization and a 25-year term. Unlike the traditional commercial loan to finance the purchase of a business with no tangible assets that will have a maximum term of five years, the SBA loan program can finance the same business over 10 years and even longer in some cases. Equipment that is typically financed over seven years with traditional commercial financing can be financed over 10 or more years under the SBA. Working capital is commonly financed over seven to 10 years with an SBA loan. The advantage of a longer term provided by an SBA loan is that your monthly payments will be lower. This makes it easier for your business to qualify for financing and also puts less stress on your business's cash flow. SBA term length will be discussed in more detail in Part Two.

7) **Investment Income**

Investment income is always a hot topic with entrepreneurs looking to purchase real estate for their businesses. The conditions to acquire real estate of which your business can generate investment income differs between conventional and SBA loan financing.

Investment Income—Conventional Commercial Financing

For business owners looking to invest in real estate, conventional lenders generally require at least a 20% to 25% injection toward the purchase price. Many business owners have difficulty coming up with this down payment amount. Purchasing investment real estate typically requires at least a 25% injection. Many business owners who rent rather than own their business real estate dislike the fact that their rent payments every month provide them with no growth of equity or ownership interest. They view paying rent the same as just throwing their money away. Based on conventional loan requirements, most tenant businesses find it difficult not only to acquire their own real estate but also to become a landlord of other businesses.

Investment Income—SBA Financing

The SBA enables business owners to purchase real estate for their businesses with up to 100% financing. Not only can you purchase real estate for your business, you can also purchase a building with additional space that can be rented to third-party tenants. This is attractive to many business owners who would like to be their own landlord and also become a landlord for other tenants of their building. To qualify for SBA financing to purchase real estate, your own business must occupy at least 51% of the real estate acquired. For businesses that are growing, the SBA provides an excellent opportunity for you to purchase a facility much larger (almost double) than the size your business currently needs. This creates an excellent opportunity for you to generate additional rental income from third-party tenants that your business can use for growth capital. A condition for approval is that the SBA requires that your business has the capacity (without rental income) to afford the entire space on a projected basis. This is usually much easier to qualify for than you might think.

8) Debt Refinance

As businesses expand and contract, many entrepreneurs use various financing vehicles to transition their business to the next phase. Over the years, business owners may find that their debt load may be less competitive than the going market rate. Others may find that their existing debt terms are causing their business financial strain. Whatever the reason, it is common for business owners to seek more favorable terms to help them reach their business growth objectives. The benefits and ability of refinancing business debt under the SBA and conventional loan programs differ.

Debt Refinance—Conventional Commercial Financing

Refinancing debt with a conventional commercial loan can be difficult. If the debt balance to be refinanced is greater than the liquidation value of the collateral, the loan amount requested will either be declined or approved with a short repayment term. Commercial loans that are not fully secured will usually require monthly payments that are too high for the business to afford, resulting in cash flow stress. For businesses that can fully secure a proposed debt refinance, historical cash flow can be a problem. Commercial lenders are careful when considering refinancing another financial company's loan because the request raises the concern that the new lender may be acquiring the existing lender's problems.

Debt Refinance—SBA Financing

Many business owners take advantage of SBA loan programs to refinance existing business debt. With an SBA loan, business owners can much more easily qualify to refinance that debt. Business debt can include real estate, equipment, working capital, lines of credit (LOC), equipment leases, landlord/tenant leases, business credit cards, seller loans, private loans, and other business-related leases and debts. Refinancing debt with an SBA loan can substantially reduce your monthly payments, thereby increasing monthly cash flow and your ability to grow your business. Refinancing debt to reduce monthly debt payments is the most common reason that business owners refinance debt with an SBA loan.

Commercial real estate mortgages are commonly refinanced with SBA loans. SBA real estate mortgages can be financed over 25 years and the business owner gets to avoid aggravation associated with conventional commercial mortgages. Equipment leases and loans are commonly refinanced with an SBA loan to take advantage of a financing term equal to the useful life of the equipment. Equipment financed conventionally is typically financed over a much shorter period of time than the period of time that your business will actually use the equipment. For example, you may acquire a printing press for your business that you can use for 15 years; however, the finance company may only be willing to provide financing or a lease agreement for five years. The SBA permits equipment to be financed over its useful life. The cash flow savings of paying for the equipment over 15 years versus five years is substantial. In addition, the five-year term could put too much stress on your business, potentially causing business failure if your business suffered from slower sales during certain periods.

9) <u>Loan Servicing</u>

Loan servicing is the loan stage after your loan is funded. It is the period of time from when your loan is funded until your loan is repaid in full. Loan servicing has become a major topic of commercial borrower stress in recent years due to increased bank regulation and ongoing compliancy tests imposed on entrepreneurs by lenders. The loan servicing requirements and imposed penalties for noncompliance differ greatly between conventional commercial loans and SBA loans.

Loan Servicing—Conventional Commercial Financing

Traditional commercial lenders have stringent requirements that must be met in order to remain in compliance with loan agreements. These include, at a minimum, a regular submission of business tax returns, personal tax returns, interim financial statements, and annual personal financial statements for all loan guarantors. The reason for these servicing requirements is so the banks can determine if you and your business continue to meet the financial covenants specified in the loan agreements and so that the banks can continually evaluate their loan risk with your business. If the bank is concerned about your business, it may require you to order and provide reports such as field audits, which can cost several thousand dollars. These expenses are billed to you. For businesses that do several million dollars in sales, audited financials are usually required in which a CPA firm will certify that the financials have been prepared to meet generally accepted accounting procedures (GAAP) and whether the company is in compliance with loan covenants. All of these servicing requirements are extremely time consuming and expensive for business owners. Audited financials can cost more than $30,000 annually. They also create a potential liability to the business if the bank determines that it doesn't like something and wants to be paid off. For any servicing actions, such as if you want to change a condition of your loan like your interest rate, collateral, or some other type of modification, you should be prepared to pay fees.

Loan Servicing—SBA Financing

On the SBA side, annual submission of tax returns and other financial information is required; however, if you have consistently made your payments as agreed, the intrusion on your business is limited to this requirement. If you want to request a modification of some term of the existing loan, such as the release of collateral to be replaced by other collateral, no fees are allowed to be charged by the lender. The lender is also unable to request immediate repayment or change any terms without your consent throughout the term of the loan. Other than the requirement to provide annual financial information (and to make your payments!), compliance with the terms of the SBA loans is really simple, much like your home loan. Annual financial information enables the SBA lender to assist you with expansion opportunities, modifications, or financial challenges during the term of the loan.

10) <u>Amortization</u>

Amortization is the period of time over which your loan payments are calculated. For instance, home loans are typically amortized over 30 years, meaning that if you make 30 years of payments, your loan will be fully repaid.

Amortization—Conventional Commercial Financing

The typical residential repayment structure of making mortgage payments until the loan is repaid in full is not typical for commercial mortgages. Most commercial (business) loans require you, the borrower, to periodically requalify for your business loan (or to refinance your loan). For example, most conventional commercial loans contain a balloon payment provision. The most common period (term) is five years, meaning that the loan balance will come due (balloon) at the end of the five-year term. Based on a 25-year amortization schedule and five-year term, you will have to qualify for your commercial loan at least five times before it is paid off. Traditionally, the bank will offer you a fixed or variable interest rate for a term of five years. After the five years, the bank will again collect all of your application information to analyze if you and your business are still an acceptable risk to the bank. If you do not qualify, you are forced to quickly find a new source of financing. This gives the bank the opportunity to spend your money to order new reports such as appraisals, searches, credit reports, financial audits, etc. In addition, the bank may charge you renewal fees to extend the term of your loan. Your existing lender knows that you will have to pay origination fees if you refinance your loan with another lender and therefore can charge you its own fees (at a slight discount) and keep you. Commercial borrowers hate having to continually requalify for their business financing because it's a hassle, time consuming, stressful, and often expensive.

Amortization—SBA Financing

Unlike traditional commercial loans, the SBA loan programs were designed to be much more similar to the typical 15- or 30-year residential mortgage that you are probably familiar with. The SBA wants you to feel at ease so that you can just focus on making your monthly payments, and your loan will eventually be paid in full without you ever having to requalify or refinance the balance unless you choose to do so. If you are purchasing a commercial property with an SBA loan and offered 25 years to repay your loan, your payments will be based on a 25-year amortization schedule, and you can continue making payments for 25 years. If you never make any additional principal payments to speed up your repayment, you will make the same monthly payment for 25 years, after which time your loan would be repaid in full. If you apply for financing to purchase a business and are offered a 10-year amortization, likewise you will have 10 years to pay off the business loan.

The comfort of knowing that you will never be forced out of an SBA loan on which you have continually and consistently made the required monthly payments is a huge advantage over conventional commercial financing options.

11) Intangible Asset Financing

Intangible assets are assets owned by a business that are much more difficult to sell in a liquidation proceeding than hard assets such as real estate or equipment. Examples of intangible assets include goodwill, leasehold improvements, licenses, and soft costs such as closing costs and permits. The ability to finance intangible assets varies greatly between conventional and SBA loan programs.

Intangible Asset Financing—Conventional Commercial Financing

Intangible assets are very difficult to be financed through conventional loan programs. They are difficult to finance because much of their value is dependent on a viable business. Two examples of intangible assets are leasehold improvements (also called tenant finish) and goodwill. An example of a leasehold improvement is a wall that you build in your leased office space. This new wall may benefit your landlord's real estate value but is of little value to a lender for collateral as it cannot be sold if your business were to fail. Goodwill is also difficult to finance in that the collateral value of the goodwill is dependent on the ability of your business to remain viable. If the business fails, most of the goodwill will be lost unless the lender is able to quickly reopen your business to continue generating positive cash flow. As you can imagine, conventional lenders do not put much value on intangible assets, so they rarely lend against them. The best-case scenario is seven-year financing, but finding something longer than three to five years without the SBA is only available for extremely strong companies.

Intangible Asset Financing—SBA Financing

One of the primary reasons the SBA created its loan programs was to fill this huge intangible asset financing void. If you think about every shopping center full of businesses leasing their space, many of these units would be vacant if it wasn't for the SBA. An SBA loan is a great option for those interested in purchasing a business, obtaining financing for a business that will be leasing space, starting a franchise business, or obtaining any other business financing that is not fully secured by real estate or other tangible assets. A huge advantage of SBA financing over conventional business financing is that intangible assets such as goodwill and leasehold improvements can be financed with an SBA loan.

CHAPTER 2

WHY YOU WANT AN SBA LOAN: REASONS 12-21

In this chapter we'll continue our discussion of why you want an SBA loan. We pick up with reason number 12.

12) <u>High-Risk Industries</u>

High-risk industries include businesses that typically have a high-default rate. This means that if you are applying for financing for a business in a high-risk industry, statistics show that loan default is more likely. To maintain a strong loan portfolio and avoid "problem credits", most lenders are careful when lending to businesses in high-risk industries.

High-Risk Industries—Conventional Commercial Financing

Banks and finance companies make money by lending money; however, they tend to target industries with low risk. The most common example of an industry that most conventional lenders avoid is the food and beverage industry. Restaurants come and go and have one of the highest default rates. Another industry that is difficult to obtain conventional financing for is the hospitality industry. Hospitality businesses such as hotels and motels are heavily reliant on transient customers traveling for vacation or business. The recent economic downturn of 2008 to 2010 dramatically impacted this industry. Many high-risk businesses also occupy special- purpose properties. Special-purpose properties are properties that are not easily converted to a use other than what they were originally designed to accommodate. Examples of special- purpose properties include gas stations, car washes, and bowling alleys. Banks and finance companies prefer to finance commercial real estate, including multifamily buildings, office buildings, industrial buildings, and retail buildings, as these spaces can accommodate or be easily converted to accommodate a wide variety of businesses and tenants.

High-Risk Industries—SBA Financing

Under the SBA, high-risk industries are more easily financed. Examples of high-risk businesses more easily financed include restaurants and businesses that occupy special-purpose properties such as a car wash. Not only are these properties eligible to be financed with SBA financing, you are likely to get a much higher LTV than under conventional bank options. Environmentally risky businesses such as gas stations do require additional environmental screening; however, these requirements are there to protect you, the SBA lender, and the SBA from acquiring a property that is contaminated. Contaminated properties are very difficult to finance until they have been cleaned, which can cost hundreds of thousands of dollars.

13) <u>Multi-Purpose Loans</u>

Multi-purpose loans are loans that satisfy multiple uses of the funds. All loan requests combine at least two uses of loan proceeds including the primary purpose such as a real estate purchase and the closing costs associated with the real estate loan request. How multi-purpose loans are financed differ between conventional and SBA loan programs.

Multi-Purpose Loans—Conventional Commercial Financing

When you apply for financing through conventional loan vehicles, the bank or finance company is likely to offer individual loans for each of your requests and exclude closing costs from eligible loan proceeds. If you want to purchase a building, buy inventory, upgrade your equipment, and get some working capital, the lender is likely to offer you four loans, each with its own terms, conditions, and monthly invoices. Most entrepreneurs like their accounts to be simple, so having four loans can be inconvenient. Approval from four different divisions of the bank may also be required in those situations, causing delay and confusion.

Multi-Purpose Loans—SBA Financing

Under the SBA, it is most common to have several loan purposes and uses under a single loan agreement to keep things simple. If you were to apply for financing to purchase a building, buy inventory, replace equipment, and get some additional working capital, everything can be bundled together giving you one loan, one payment, and one agreement to follow. In addition, the closing costs associated with the loan would be included in the financing package, reducing your out-of-pocket expense.

14) Balloon Payments

A balloon, also known as "mortgage balloon," is the expiration date or maturity date of your business loan. Balloons provide lenders the ability to renegotiate existing terms of your loan at this maturity date, including forcing you out of the bank if the existing bank no longer wants your business. Balloons are scary because your financing is only temporary unlike your typical home loan. Balloons are perceived differently under conventional and SBA loan programs.

Balloons—Conventional Commercial Financing

Most conventional commercial mortgage loans are approved with a repayment term that is shorter than the amortization period on which the payments are based. For example, a conventional commercial real estate loan is typically approved with a 20-year amortization. This means that your payments will be based on a repayment period of 20 years. Although the loan may be based on a 20-year repayment period, the entire unpaid balance will be due in five years. The five-year balloon condition means that after making timely monthly payments for five years based on the 20-year schedule, the then-entire unpaid balance is due. This is when the balloon pops. This forces business owners and commercial real estate borrowers to refinance or requalify their loans every five years. Refinancing commercial loans is stressful, expensive, and time consuming.

Balloons—SBA Financing

The SBA has determined that loans with balloons are unreasonable because they force the borrower to requalify or refinance their existing loan. The SBA term loan programs such as the SBA 7(a) and SBA 504, have loan terms that match the amortization. This provides borrowers with stability and assurance that they never need to refinance their loan if they don't want to. With an SBA loan, you can make your monthly payments every month for the term of the loan, and eventually your loan will be repaid in full just like a traditional 15- or 30-year residential mortgage.

15) Demand Loans

Demand loans are designed to give lenders the ability to make changes to the existing terms of your loan if certain requirements are not met. If certain requirements are not met, such as not providing annual financial statements within a specified time, your loan can be flagged as in default, at which time the lender can change your loan terms up to and including demanding immediate repayment. Conventional lenders and the SBA have different demand loan requirements.

Demand Loans—Conventional Commercial Financing

One of the scariest provisions of conventional commercial loans is the "on demand" provision. The "on demand" provision enables lenders to demand repayment of your business loan at any time based on provisions in the loan closing documents that you are unlikely to be aware of. The most common conditions linked to "on demand" are debt service covenants, profitability covenants, leverage covenants, and timely financial reporting. Most businesses suffered in 2008, 2009, and 2010 during the recession, enabling banks to enforce their rights under the loan agreements and demand immediate repayment of the commercial loans. Many businesses that were affected by the downturn in the economy first had to adjust to the economy and then, second, had to go into emergency mode when their banks demanded immediate repayment of their loans.

There are several conditions that accompany conventional commercial loans that must be met during the term of the loan. Failure to meet any of these conditions enables the lender to notify you that your loan is in default, at which time the lender can change the terms of your loan including demanding immediate repayment of the loan. Most lenders require demand notes on their loans so that if they feel that repayment of their loan is at risk, they can demand immediate repayment and charge additional fees. Repayment of your loan may have always been made on time and as agreed; however, if any of your covenants were not met, the lender can demand repayment, forcing you to look for alternative financing in short order. Many demand notes are actually written so that the lender can demand repayment at any time and for any reason.

Demand Loans—SBA Financing

SBA lenders are restricted from making demand of your SBA loan. SBA lenders can only "demand" immediate repayment of your loan if you have defaulted in repayment and the SBA concurs that demanding immediate repayment is the only option. The SBA is far more concerned about your ability to make your payment than what your tax returns and financial statements look like on an annual basis. The SBA considers to be unreasonable any loan that can be "demanded" to be repaid in full at any time due to leverage covenants and cash flow covenants. Repayment of your loan is your responsibility, and the SBA believes that if you can find a way to make timely payments regardless of the ups and down in your businesses, you will find a way. This speaks more to your character than your evolving financial situation.

The SBA believes that the lender should be in the boat with you both in good and in bad times. If you were qualified to get the SBA loan at time of application, then you should be able to have your SBA loan until it is paid off regardless of your financial conditions. If you make your payments, there should be no reason that the lender should be able to attempt to retract its loan to you. If you miss a payment or are having cash flow troubles, the SBA wants the lender to find temporary solutions, such as interest only payments for a period of time, in an attempt to help get you back on your feet. Lenders can actually be penalized by the SBA if they attempt to enforce "on demand" provisions. Only if the SBA and the SBA lender determine that business recovery is unlikely will they move forward with liquidation. The SBA's mission is to help entrepreneurs start, build, and grow viable businesses. The SBA wants your business to be successful.

16) Closing Costs

For almost every type of loan, closing costs are an additional expense to be incurred by the borrower when obtaining any type of business financing. No one likes paying closing costs, and this additional expense can make many transactions unaffordable for many business owners attempting to obtain business financing. Closing costs impact conventional and SBA loans differently.

Closing Costs and Fees—Conventional Commercial Financing

Traditional commercial loans are required to be fully secured, forcing borrowers to inject large down payments (equity) and cover closing expenses out of pocket. For example, a real estate purchase for $1 million will typically require an equity injection of at least $200,000 plus closing costs. Closing costs typically include a bank origination fee of 1% of the amount borrowed ($8,000 in this example), a real estate appraisal with an average cost of $3,500, environmental searches which typically start around $1,500 (assuming that no adverse environmental problems exist), title costs of four-tenths of a percent ($3,200 in this example), real estate transfer taxes, attorney fees, and other fees. Closing costs can quickly add up to 2% of the loan amount ($20,000) or more. Having to come up with approximately $220,000 to purchase a million-dollar property is likely to be a financial strain on any business. In addition, every time you, the borrower, are required to requalify to keep the loan or wish to refinance the loan, many of these closing costs will again be charged and incurred. This can really add up over 20 to 25 years.

Closing Costs and Fees—SBA Financing

While closing costs and fees cannot be avoided regardless of the type of loan, for SBA loans it is customary to roll closing costs into the total project cost. Once the closing costs have been added to the total project cost, the SBA lender will then only require a minimal equity contribution percentage from the borrower. This saves you substantial working capital that is critical to the success of your business. The upfront closing costs for SBA loans are slightly higher than traditional commercial loans due to the SBA guaranty fee; however, most closing costs will never be incurred by your business ever again should you not refinance out of your SBA loan. Not having to pay closing costs ever again is a major advantage over conventional financing, as a new appraisal, renewal fees, and other bank mandated fess on the conventional loan side can really add up when they are charged at least every five years. For most SBA loans for the purpose of financing commercial real estate, SBA lenders only require a 10% injection of the total project amount. After the 10% injection, your timely monthly payment is your only responsibility until the loan is paid in full. The higher loan to value, working capital savings, ability to roll in closing costs, and other SBA loan benefits discussed in this Part are well worth the SBA guaranty fees.

17) Personal Guaranties

Personal guaranties are required for most commercial and residential loans. Providing a personal guaranty makes the individuals personally responsible for the loan regardless of the entity of which the loan is made. Requiring a personal guaranty substantially reduces the risk of loan default as it is much more difficult to walk away from debt if the business is failing. The requirements for who has to provide a personal guaranty differs between conventional and SBA loan programs.

Personal Guaranties—Conventional Commercial Financing

Most commercial lenders require loans to be guarantied by 100% of the owners of the applicant company regardless of each of their ownership percentage. Conventional loans not requiring 100% of the owners to personally guaranty the loan are only offered to commercial loan borrowers that are considered to be of low risk due to excellent cash flow, a low debt-to-collateral ratio, and other strong credit factors that mitigate loan risk. Personal guaranties are typically the bank's third option for collection in a default situation. If a business fails so that income is no longer sufficient to cover debt payments, a lender will foreclose on the collateral property and sell other business assets in an attempt to recover the outstanding loan balance plus its fees and expenses. Foreclosures are expensive and typically result in the lender not being able to collect all of the money that is due. In these cases, the lender will enforce its rights to go after the personal guarantors for the difference.

Personal Guaranties—SBA Financing

Under an SBA loan, a personal guaranty is required of owners of 20% or greater of the company. Twenty percent or greater owners are considered to have power of control over the applicant business. For this reason they are required to personally guaranty the loan. In some cases lenders may require minority owners to guaranty SBA loans; however, this is rare. This enables applicant businesses to obtain minority share investors to invest in their businesses without those investors having to personally guaranty the loan(s). Minority share owners with substantial assets are unlikely to want to provide their personal guaranty. The SBA's 20% rule can protect them and help you get their investment. This creates a win-win for everyone.

18) Prepayment Penalties

Prepayment penalties are fees that may be charged by a lender if you make larger payments than what is minimally required. Prepayment penalties are imposed by lenders so that they can predict and help preserve their interest income expected to be received during the term of your loan. Convention loan providers and the SBA have differing views about prepayment penalties.

Prepayment Penalties—Conventional Commercial Financing

Conventional loans (non-SBA) are made by banks and finance companies for the purpose of generating interest and fee income. The lender's goal is to collect all of the interest based on the term and amortization schedule that you were provided with the loan. When a borrower prepays the principal balance by making additional principal payments, the bank loses interest income. Most lenders discourage prepayment by assessing prepayment penalties in the event of prepayment of principal. Even payment of several dollars, in addition to the required monthly payment, can result in a penalty. Common types of prepayment penalties used by conventional lenders include declining prepayment penalties, yield maintenance fees, and swap breakage fees. Prepayment penalties can be substantial, making it difficult to reduce your interest expense.

Prepayment Penalties—SBA Financing

Many business owners take advantage of SBA loan programs because of their lack of prepayment penalties or actually their lack of stringent prepayment penalties. Under the SBA's primary loan program called the SBA 7(a) program, there are no prepayment penalties for loans with a term of less than 15 years. This means that you can prepay the loan as quickly as you want without penalty. If you are going to prepay more than 20% of the unpaid principal balance in any one year, you are required to simply give your lender written notice, and the lender will help you with properly applying the additional principal payment. Notice is required because many SBA loans, like residential mortgages, are sold on the secondary market, and investors need to be notified.

For SBA 7(a) loans with a term of 15 years or more, there *is* a prepayment penalty fee if you pay 25% or more of the original loan balance in the first three years. The fee is 5% of the prepayment amount during the first year, 3% the second year, and 1% in the third year. Like SBA 7(a) loans with terms less than 15 years, the lender must be notified in writing if more than 20% of the principal balance is to be paid in any one year. Prepayments of up to 20% require no notification.

Before making any principal prepayment, I advise you to speak to your CPA and/or financial advisor. Your advisor can help you determine if using working capital to reduce your loan balance, and thereby saving long-term interest expenses, is better than saving the capital for working capital purposes of your business or alternative external investments. Many advisors recommend alternative financial and investment vehicles that will generate a higher rate of return than the interest you are paying on your SBA loan or other business loan. Your CPA will help you evaluate the working capital needs of your business, interest rate risk, and alternative investment options suggested by your financial advisor. The great thing about SBA's minimal prepayment penalty is that you have the opportunity to choose what is best for you and your business. If getting out of debt quickly is your objective, the SBA enables this option.

19) <u>Stock Sales</u>

Stock sales are used to change ownership of an existing company without impacting the legal entity structure. For instance, if there are two individual 50% owners of ABC Daycare, Inc., and one of the owners wants to purchase the other owner's 50% ownership interest in ABC Daycare, Inc., they can do this through a stock sale. ABC Daycare, Inc. continues to exist after the partnership buyout; however, the ownership changes from two 50% owners to one 100% owner. Obtaining financing to perform a stock sale will be conducted differently under the conventional loan program versus the SBA loan program.

Stock Sales—Conventional Commercial Financing

Stock sales are typically not financed through traditional bank financing due to inadequate collateral. Banks are much more comfortable lending against tangible assets such as a building or equipment versus the value of the corporate stock, which can be highly volatile. Stock sales are typically financed only if the loan will be fully secured by assets other than the perceived market value of the stock. In cases where the company stock is publicly traded, debt may be offered to finance a portion of the stock sale; however, a large equity injection will be required by the buyer.

Stock Sales—SBA Financing

Stock sales are eligible for SBA financing and occur regularly. The value of the business stock is determined through a business valuation, much like how real estate is appraised for a real estate transaction. Up to 100% of the stock purchase price can be financed if it is supported by the business valuation; however, 75% financing is typical.

In circumstances where supplier and customer contracts are tied to a business entity, having the ability to perform a stock sale through the SBA enables the company sale to occur. Prior to entering into a business sale agreement, make sure that the business does not have contracts with customers and suppliers that will be lost upon sale of the business and/or change of entity. If a contract is critical to the success of a business and it will go away with the change in ownership, do not purchase the business regardless of the strength of the existing cash flow.

20) Use of Proceeds

Use of proceeds is how all money collected to perform a transaction will be used. The obvious use of proceeds is the purpose of the loan request such as to purchase real estate. The less obvious uses of proceeds include all of the transactional costs related to financing the requested loan purpose. Having several uses of proceeds including transaction costs (closing costs) may be limited depending on the type of loan requested. Conventional and SBA loan programs may differ in their limitation of use of proceeds.

Use of Proceeds—Conventional Commercial Financing

Conventional commercial loans are typically advanced with limited allowable uses of proceeds. Conventional loan proceeds are typically limited to the acquisition and improvement of real estate and equipment and for working capital. If you want to purchase a building, you can traditionally borrow up to an 80% loan to value for the purchase of the real estate. In addition to financing the purchase of real estate, there are several expenses that are incurred such as architect fees, renovation expenses, real estate transfer taxes, loan fees, and other closing costs. These additional expenses are typically not included as proceeds of the loan for the traditional lender as the loan amount is limited to 80% LTV. The borrower is responsible for covering the 20% down payment plus these other expenses. Like real estate, equipment is financed based on its own LTV requirements and conditions to secure the lender. Working capital is also advanced based on an acceptable collateral risk determined by the lender. Any costs or expenses above the acceptable collateral LTV is to be covered by the borrower.

Use of Proceeds—SBA Financing

Unlike traditional commercial loans, SBA loans can be used for almost any purpose that benefits the applicant's business. SBA loan proceeds can be used to purchase land, buildings, and improvements, construct a building, add an addition to a building, make renovations to a building, pay off interim construction loans, pay off interim loans, make leasehold improvements to a building, purchase machinery and equipment, purchase fixtures, purchase inventory, pay trade or accounts payable, pay notes payable, pay outstanding debt, purchase a business, purchase all outstanding stock of a company, acquire intangible assets, pay off an SBA loan, use for working capital, pay the SBA guaranty fee, pay soft costs such as engineering fees and other closing costs, and other applicant business expenses. SBA loans can be used for more purposes and with fewer restrictions. Under the SBA 7(a) program, use of proceeds is also not restricted by collateral.

21) Franchise Financing

Owning a franchise business can be a great option for entrepreneurs who want to run their own business without having to figure everything out on their own. Much of the planning and issues of running the business have been completed by others. Franchise licenses come with an instruction manual and training, so there is very little that you need to figure out on your own. This can save a substantial amount of money, time, and potential business failure as compared to opening a non-franchise start-up business.

Franchise Financing—Conventional Commercial Financing

The challenge with most franchise businesses is that they typically require an investment in intangible assets that are difficult to finance under conventional terms. Most franchise businesses also operate out of leased space providing no real estate collateral to secure the loan. This makes it ineligible for traditional financing that requires real estate collateral. The improvements that the franchise company requires you to make instantly gives your new franchise business value as your target market is likely to be familiar with the brand and tenant finish design; however, the wall covering and franchise specific equipment are generally of little value to lenders as collateral.

Franchise Financing—SBA Financing

Unlike traditional financing options, the SBA strongly supports franchise financing. Obtaining financing for a franchise company is typically much easier than obtaining a start-up loan for a non-franchise company. The reason for this is that each franchise on the SBA franchise registry is analyzed at least annually, and the analysis provides predictive information as to the likelihood of default. This information provides lenders and the SBA with much more comfort in the potential success of a new franchise business. Due to the strength of the franchise brand and national oversight by the franchisor, much of the start-up risk is mitigated. Under the SBA, all costs related to starting, purchasing, or expanding an approved franchise concept are eligible to be financed. These costs include franchise fees, attorney fees, architect fees, furniture, fixtures, equipment, leasehold improvements (tenant finish), working capital, inventory, goodwill, and more. In addition, franchise businesses can be financed over a term of at least 10 years. Every year, the SBA reviews thousands of franchise concepts for approval for financing under the SBA loan programs. Approved franchises are listed at www.franchiseregistry.com.

PART TWO
SBA TERMS, CONDITIONS, AND ELIGIBILITY

Whenever someone is considering an SBA loan or really any type of loan, it's common to have questions. The most frequently asked questions have to do with eligibility, terms, and loan conditions. It's a good idea to know the ins and outs of any loan program you are considering. To address these frequently asked questions, this section has been divided into three chapters. This section is jam-packed with straightforward information that will help you qualify for SBA financing regardless of your circumstances.

In Chapter 3, an overview of the four most popular SBA loan programs is discussed from smallest to largest. These loan programs include the SBA Microloan, the SBA Express loan, the SBA 7(a) loan, and the SBA 504 loan. Chapter 4 is all about SBA loan eligibility. This chapter was written from the SBA 7(a) loan program perspective, on which most of the other programs are based. This chapter was also written in a Q&A format enabling you to search for the information most relevant to your needs. You will quickly learn that most businesses qualify for SBA financing. Chapter 5 is all about SBA terms and conditions and closely resembles Chapter 4 with questions and answers. Chapter 5 was also written based on the SBA 7(a) loan program.

From the time you start to develop your loan request, through the time your loan is submitted to underwriting, and even up through after closing, these chapters were designed to provide a source of reference for the SBA loan programs.

CHAPTER 3

TYPES OF SBA LOANS AVAILABLE

What SBA loan programs are available for my business?

There are several SBA loan programs that you may be offered by your SBA lender to meet your funding request. I'm not going to discuss all of them and overwhelm you. Instead, I am going to highlight the features of several of the most commonly offered programs that meet the needs of 99% of the business community. If your unique circumstances fall outside the guidelines of these particular programs, rest assured that the foundation of knowledge and application worksheets detailed in this book are applicable to all SBA programs.

The four SBA loan programs to be discussed are the SBA Microloan program, the SBA Express loan program, the SBA 7(a) loan program, and the SBA 504 loan program. To reduce confusion, I have written this book from the SBA 7(a) loan program perspective. The SBA 7(a) program is the basis for almost all SBA loan programs, including eligibility requirements.

What are SBA Microloans?

Microloans are small loans of up to $50,000. These loans are provided by nonprofit community-based intermediary lenders within assigned territories (counties and zip codes) across the United States. Loan proceeds can be used for working capital, acquisition of machinery and equipment, inventory purchases, and leasehold improvements. Loan proceeds cannot be used to purchase real estate. Eligibility requirements are the same as the SBA 7(a) loan program. These loans have a maximum maturity of six years. This is the recommended program for business loan requests of up to $50,000. To find a microloan provider in your area, visit www.ApprovedBook.com.

What is an SBA Express loan?
The SBA Express program is a streamlined SBA loan program for loans and lines of credit of up to $350,000. SBA Express loans provide lenders with a maximum SBA guaranty of 50%. SBA eligibility is based on requirements discussed in this Part. For smaller and less complex transactions, SBA lenders may decide to offer an SBA Express loan instead of a standard SBA 7(a) loan or other type of loan.

It is common for SBA Express loans to be offered as a companion to an SBA 7(a) loan for working capital purposes. SBA Express loans are often offered for new businesses, expanding businesses, or businesses that have accounts receivable. An SBA Express loan offered as a line of credit will typically have a seven-year maturity. For up to three years, you will be able to borrow against the line of credit up to the credit limit. The line of credit will then convert to a term loan to be repaid with principal and interest payments over the remaining term of the seven years. A benefit of SBA Express loans offered as a line of credit is that the SBA prohibits lenders from charging renewal fees as lenders typically do on conventional commercial lines of credit.

What is an SBA 7(a) loan?
The SBA 7(a) loan program is the agency's most popular loan program based on dollars funded and number of loans made. For the 12-month SBA fiscal year ending September 30, 2013, over $18 billion of SBA 7(a) loans were approved for small businesses across the United States. The SBA 7(a) loan program is an excellent option for loan requests ranging from $50,000 to $5 million. Due to the popularity of this program, the terms, conditions, and eligibility

requirements of the SBA 7(a) loan program will be discussed in detail following this program overview.

What is an SBA 504 loan?

The SBA 504 loan program is the agency's second largest loan program based on dollars funded. Funds borrowed under the SBA 504 loan program are restricted to real estate and heavy equipment. The program has a unique loan structure in that it involves a first mortgage and second mortgage. The first mortgage is a conventional loan with a loan to value representing at least 50% of the total project amount. The second mortgage is a loan amount guarantied by the SBA that represents up to 40% of the total project amount. A minimum equity injection of 10% is required. An additional 5% equity injection is required for start-up businesses and for real estate properties that have been determined to be "special purpose." This is the SBA's premier economic development program to facilitate job creation and strengthen the economy. This program is usually recommended for real estate or heavy equipment purchase loan requests ranging from $1 million to more than $10 million.

What is the best SBA loan program for my business?

To streamline the SBA loan program selection process, the programs have been divided based on loan request size. Your loan request will fall under one of four loan size brackets:

1. Up to $50,000;
2. Between $50,000 and $350,000;
3. Greater than $350,000 and up to $5 million; or
4. Greater than $5 million.

For loans under $50,000, I recommend that you reach out to one of your local microloan providers. A complete list is available at www.ApprovedBook. com. Microloans are an excellent option for these small loans. For loans up to $350,000, either the SBA 7(a) or the SBA Express loan is recommended. For loans in excess of $350,000 and up to $5 million, the SBA 7(a) loan is the preferred program for most SBA loan requests. The SBA 7(a) loan program is also the standard program when loan proceeds are to be used for several purposes simultaneously such as a business acquisition and real estate purchase. For loan requests over $5 million, your request cannot be provided solely by an SBA 7(a) option, so a combination of SBA 7(a) and SBA 504 or just an SBA 504 should be considered. For most SBA loan requests, the SBA 7(a) loan program is the agency's most commonly offered program.

CHAPTER 4

SBA 7(A) LOAN ELIGIBILITY

What are the eligibility requirements for SBA financing?
In this chapter, we will discuss eligibility for the various SBA loan programs; however, we will primarily be discussing eligibility from the SBA 7(a) loan program perspective because it is the flagship program of the Small Business Administration. Topics will be discussed in a question and answer format to best address eligibility from your perspective.

Who is eligible for an SBA loan?
To be eligible to receive SBA financing, the applicant must meet several eligibility requirements. The eligibility requirements are:

1. The small business applicant must be an operating business;
2. The business must be organized for profit;
3. The business must be located in the United States;
4. The applicant business must be "small" as defined by SBA;
5. The applicant must demonstrate a need for the desired SBA loan;

6. The lender must certify that the loan cannot be made on "reasonable terms" without the SBA's assistance; and

7. The applicant business must not be a business that is specifically identified as an ineligible business.

What is an "operating business"?

An operating business is a business that is actively managed or operated. It can be an existing business or a start-up. Upon receipt of the SBA loan proceeds and applicant's contribution, the start-up business will be considered to be an operating business. An operating business is not a passive business such as an investment property in which the owner (landlord) just collects rent and is not actively running the business on a daily basis.

What is a "small business"?

SBA loan applicants must be "small" based on the SBA's size guidelines and restrictions. Over the years, what the SBA deems to be "small" has increased markedly. It has also become easier to determine. Most SBA lenders use the "alternative size standard rule," which is a much more straightforward method to determine "size" eligibility.

What is the "alternative size standard rule"?

To qualify under the alternative size standard, the applicant business (including affiliates, if any) must:

1. Have a maximum tangible net worth not exceeding $15 million, *and*

2. Have an average net income after federal income taxes (excluding any carry-over losses) not exceeding $5 million, which is calculated based on the last two full fiscal years prior to the date of the application.

You should note that most applicants fall within the alternative size standard rule since their net income is less than $5 million. To determine if you have a tangible net worth of greater than $15 million, the SBA lender will look at your business's balance sheet. On the balance sheet you will see "assets" at the top with "total assets" listed at the bottom of the "assets" section. You will see "liabilities" below this and "total liabilities" at the bottom of the "liabilities" section. Below "total liabilities" will be "net worth," also called "equity." "Net worth" is your "total assets" minus your "total liabilities." Your "net worth" may be positive or negative on your balance sheet depending on depreciation and other factors not to worry about at this time. Back up at the top half of your balance sheet, "assets" are broken down into "tangible" and "intangible assets." If you see an amount listed for "intangible assets" in the assets section, subtract this amount from "net worth" and you will have your "tangible net worth." Having an issue with qualifying as a "small business" is rarely a problem, but if your business is too big under the alternative size standard, speak with an SBA loan expert about qualifying based on your specific industry's standard size criteria. Some industries can qualify based on number of employees, enabling large companies with strong cash flow and balance sheets to qualify.

What is an affiliate business?

The SBA has determined that affiliation can exist through common ownership, common management, excessive restrictions upon the sale/transfer of a franchise interest, and/or excessive control by a franchisor such that you, the franchisee, do not have the independent right to profit from your efforts and bear the risk of loss commensurate with ownership. As a rule of thumb, if any of the principal owners (applicants with at least a 20% ownership interest) listed on your SBA application have ownership interest in other businesses of at least 20%, those other businesses are considered to be affiliates. All affiliates are combined to determine eligibility based on size standard; however, even with ownership in several entities, it is uncommon for business applicants to exceed the maximum size standards for SBA loans.

What does it mean to "demonstrate a need for the desired SBA loan"?

The SBA provides lenders with a government guaranty to encourage them to make business loans that they otherwise would not make. If a lender would make a requested loan *without* the SBA guaranty, the SBA will not allow the lender to make the loan *with* the SBA guaranty. This would be a waste of government resources. Also, if the applicant had the cash resources to fund the requested project financing without a loan, the SBA guaranty would also be overkill. It's like asking for insurance in addition to cash security—it's frivolous. To determine a "need," the SBA created a "credit elsewhere test." Once the credit elsewhere test has been completed and it is determined that there still is a need for the SBA loan, then this requirement will be met.

What is the "credit elsewhere test"?

The "credit elsewhere test" is where the SBA lender determines that the terms and conditions that the lender will provide for the applicant without an SBA guaranty are inferior to the terms and conditions that the lender will provide with an SBA guaranty. This is a fairly easy test for a lender to meet. Many reasons were covered in Part One when we discussed advantages of SBA loans over conventional commercial loans. The SBA loan terms and conditions may be superior to conventional terms and conditions if:

- The maturity (term) is longer under the SBA than under conventional credit policy. For example, most lenders finance real estate with a five- to 10-year term, while SBA loans secured by commercial real estate are typically financed with a 25-year term. Business loans secured by intangible assets such as goodwill are extremely difficult to finance conventionally while they are commonly financed over a 10-year or longer term with an SBA loan;

- The conventional commercial lender requires the loan to be made on a demand basis or with a balloon. In most situations, the conventional loan is provided for a shorter repayment period than the period for which payments are calculated. For instance, you may receive a commercial loan of which your monthly payments are calculated based on a payment schedule (amortization) of 20 years, but your loan comes due in five years or at any time the lender wishes (on demand). In this case the SBA terms are superior;

- The collateral doesn't meet the lender's policy. Lenders are more likely to make loans secured by multi-purpose commercial real estate than special-purpose real estate or other business assets that are less easily sold in a foreclosure proceeding. When the collateral does not meet the lender's policy, the loan will be declined or the LTV is likely to be much lower. The SBA collateral requirements are typically much more favorable than traditional bank collateral requirements;

- The LTV is higher than what the lender's credit policy permits. Most lenders provide commercial real estate financing for up to 80% loan to value. If the property type is not multi-purpose, policy usually will require LTV to be as low at 50%. SBA doesn't have LTV requirements on commercial real estate once it is determined that the loan cannot be fully secured;

- The loan amount is greater than the bank's lending authority. For smaller banks, making SBA loans may provide them the ability to make larger loans than they are legally able to make without government assistance. A guaranteed loan may allow a bank to offer commercial financing by up to 4x the amount their legal lending authority allows;

- The bank must offer guaranteed loans that can be sold to preserve liquidity. Many smaller banks cannot afford to make loans if they cannot quickly recoup the loan proceeds to make additional loans. Like most home loans that are sold on the secondary market, SBA loans enable a lender to sell the guaranteed portion to recoup 75% of the original loan amount;

- The lender doesn't finance new businesses without an SBA guaranty. Banks avoid making loans to businesses that are considered to be risky, such as start-up companies. The guaranty provided by the SBA reduces the risk by providing a guaranty for a portion of the loan. For example, a $400,000 SBA loan will have a 75% guaranty so the lender would only be at risk for $100,000 versus $400,000. This reduced risk may justify the bank to make the start-up loan considering the upside of collecting interest income on $400,000 while having a risk of only $100,000;

- The lender doesn't typically make loans to businesses within the applicant's industry. Commercial lenders regularly review internal and external reports detailing economic expectations by industry, industry performance historically, and other industry predictive information. It is common for lenders to have blacklists for specific industries: restaurants, gas stations, and hotel-like properties are examples of businesses that are frequently blacklisted. An SBA guaranty may mitigate blacklisting a business within a particular industry;

- Derogatory information on the applicant's credit report cannot be overcome without the SBA guaranty. Similar to residential lending, a derogatory credit history and credit score have a substantial impact on an applicant's ability to get financing. The SBA guaranty may make the SBA lender comfortable to look past a low credit score or derogatory credit history; and
- Several other credit profile weaknesses that can be mitigated with an SBA guaranty.

To summarize the credit elsewhere test, if the commercial lender isn't willing to offer the exact same terms and conditions on a conventional commercial basis as it would offer you with an SBA guaranty, the loan is eligible to be processed under the SBA. Most SBA lenders have a couple of boilerplate sentences that they list on thousands of SBA submissions to satisfy this SBA eligibility requirement. Many circumstances that you may believe to be too detrimental to qualify for SBA financing are eligible.

What businesses have been determined to be ineligible for SBA financing?

Most business types are eligible for SBA financing; however, there are some businesses that have been determined by SBA to be ineligible. It is unlikely that your business will be one of these, but search the list to make sure. Ineligible businesses are:

- Nonprofit businesses such as a 501(c)(3);
- Finance companies that primarily engage in the business of lending;
- Passive businesses, except eligible passive companies (EPC);
- Life insurance companies (agents are OK);

- Businesses located on foreign soil;
- Pyramid sales companies;
- Businesses deriving more than one-third of their gross income from legal gambling;
- Businesses engaged in any illegal activity;
- Private clubs and businesses that limit membership for reasons other than capacity;
- Government-owned entities;
- Religious businesses;
- Consumer and marketing cooperatives;
- SBA loan packagers;
- Businesses with an associate who is incarcerated, on probation, on parole, or has been indicted for a felony or a crime of moral turpitude;
- Businesses in which the lender or associate has an equity interest;
- Businesses that present live performances of a prurient sexual nature or sell products of which more than 5% of their gross income is of a prurient sexual nature;
- A business or applicant involved in a business that defaulted on a federal loan or federally assisted financing resulting in a loss to the government;
- Political or lobbying companies;
- Speculative businesses (such as oil wildcatting or research and development); and
- Businesses owned by non-US citizens (lawful permanent residents are eligible).

What is a passive business?

Passive businesses are businesses that are owned by developers and landlords who do not actively use or occupy the assets acquired or improved. For example, a real estate developer who purchases land to be subdivided and sold for development is not eligible. Real estate that is acquired to be leased out to unaffiliated businesses is considered to be a passive business and therefore ineligible for SBA financing. Most shopping centers (strip malls) are considered to be passive businesses and therefore ineligible. On the contrary, if you own several of the businesses in the shopping center such that your businesses occupy at least 51% of the leasable space at the shopping center, then the property itself would be eligible for SBA financing. See *eligible passive companies* for additional information.

Examples of ineligible businesses considered to be passive businesses by the SBA include apartment buildings, shopping centers, investment real estate, and cell towers. Generally all of these businesses collect income based on long-term leases and contracts; little active management is required. While an assisted living facility is similar to an apartment building in that the occupants are long term, it *is* eligible for SBA financing. An assisted living facility is eligible because it is an actively run business, the facility provides much more than rent collection, and active management is required.

What is an eligible passive company (EPC)?

Often an entrepreneur will form two or more entities for one business. This is generally done for accounting and liability purposes. It is common for a business owner to form an entity (LLC, LP, S Corp, etc.) to own real estate and a separate entity to operate the business from the real estate location. An EPC is a separate legal entity that is formed to hold the real estate financed with an SBA loan. The real estate company called the EPC can only hold title to the real estate assets. The OC (operating company) will be the entity by which you will run your business. If you have several businesses that will occupy space owned by the EPC, there will be several OCs, which is just fine with the SBA. Again, the purpose of having an EPC/OC relationship is for accounting and liability reasons. The OC will pay rent to the EPC just as if it were renting the space from a separate and independent third party. The EPC company will then use the collected rent money to pay real-estate-related expenses such as property taxes, property insurance, property maintenance, and most importantly the SBA loan mortgage payments on behalf of the operating company (OC).

This may seem to complicate your finances, however, CPAs and attorneys actually prefer this relationship because a real estate business is very different from the business of the operating company. Expenses related to real estate should be separated from the expenses related to running your business. Also, in the future if you wanted to sell your business but keep the real estate, this EPC/OC relationship would already be set up, enabling you to easily separate the two entities. On the liability side, if someone were to slip and fall and file a lawsuit against the operating business, the real estate assets would be protected from the lawsuit as the business entity wouldn't own the real estate. Only the assets of the operating company would be subject to the lawsuit. Obviously your liability insurance policy for the business should be adequate to protect your business assets from a lawsuit; however, in the litigious society in which we live, additional protection by using the EPC/OC structure adds a second layer of protection.

An example of an EPC/OC is a daycare business that owns the real estate that the daycare occupies. The real estate is held under a company called "Day Care Real Estate, LLC" and the business is operated under the name of "ABC Daycare, LLC." The website and signage all over the building displays the name as "ABC Daycare," as this is the business name.

There are specific SBA requirements that must be met for an EPC/OC relationship to be in compliance prior to the SBA loan closing; however, a qualified SBA professional can and will assist with this. The most important requirement is that the rent paid by the OC to the EPC is not excessive, meaning that the rent payments are not greater than what is necessary to cover loan payments and real-estate-related expenses such as taxes, insurance, and maintenance. The SBA wants the OC to be in control of the business's capital, especially in cases where it appears that the owner of the EPC company appears more interested in collecting excess rent and distributing net income to the owners of the EPC rather than meeting the working capital needs of the tenant business (OC).

What can SBA loan proceeds be used for?

SBA loan proceeds can be used for just about anything that a business applicant would request. The official list of eligible SBA uses of proceeds is:

- Permanent working capital;
- Revolving working capital;
- Furniture and fixtures;

- Machinery and equipment, including installation;
- Purchase of land and building, including construction and renovations;
- Business acquisition; and
- Refinancing of existing debt.

Although this list appears to be short and missing several things, the items on it are intended to be general. For example, purchasing inventory is a common use of SBA loan proceeds and is not specifically listed. The "Use of Proceeds" worksheet discussed in Part Five provides the expanded list of what is detailed above.

What can SBA loan proceeds NOT be used for?

There are only a few circumstances in which the proposed use of SBA loan proceeds have been determined to be ineligible. SBA proceeds cannot be used to:

- Provide cash out of equity in a business without a specific future business use;
- Provide floor plan financing;
- Invest in real or personal property acquired and held primarily for sale, lease, or investment that does not meets the requirements of EPC/OC;
- Pay delinquent taxes including withholding (payroll) taxes and sales taxes; and
- Relocate a business out of a community which would cause more damage to that community than the benefit to the company and the receiving community.

Can SBA funds be used to refinance existing debt?

It is common to use SBA proceeds to refinance existing debt. For debt to be refinanced the existing debt must be on "unreasonable terms" and the new SBA loan payments generally must be at least 10% less than the existing monthly payment amounts.

Your debt will be considered to be on "unreasonable terms" by SBA criteria if it is:

- Debt with an interest rate that exceeds the current SBA maximum interest rate;
- Debt that is over-collateralized;
- Debt with a maturity that was not appropriate for the purpose of the financing (useful life);
- Debt used to finance a change of ownership; or
- Debt the SBA lender believes no longer meets the needs of the small business applicant.

There are also three types of debt the SBA deems to be unreasonable which are not subject to the 10% savings rule. If your existing debt meets *any* of the following terms, you don't need to show the 10% savings and your debt is eligible for SBA refinancing. These are:

1. Short- or long-term debt structured with a demand note or balloon payment;
2. Credit card obligations used for business-related purposes; and
3. Revolving lines of credit (short or long term) which the original lender is unwilling to renew, or the applicant wishes to restructure its financing in order to obtain a lower interest rate and/or longer term.

Most commercial term loans and commercial mortgage loans are determined to be on "unreasonable terms" because of either the demand note or balloon payment provision. A demand note is a loan agreement in which the lender can demand repayment of the loan in its entirety at any time for a reason other than not making your payments. A common example of this is when a bank determines that your cash flow doesn't meet the debt coverage ratio covenant (requirement) that it has set and calls your loan then due and payable as a result. With instability, uncertainty, and frequent changes in the economy, adverse weather conditions, local construction, competition and the like, it is easy for businesses to have cycles of good and bad months. Many business owners discovered the ugly side of these demand notes during the recent recession when their bank called their loans immediately due. If you are not aware of a "demand note" provision because it is not highlighted in your commercial loan note, it is usually hidden in the fine print. This provision enables most commercial loan notes to meet SBA's eligibility requirement to be refinanced.

Balloon payments are also standard with conventional financing. A loan has a balloon payment if the balance of the loan is due and payable in full prior to the time the loan is fully amortized. It's common for banks to offer business owners a five-year fixed rate based on a 20-year amortization schedule. In this common scenario, the loan will have to be refinanced or renegotiated after the five-year period. Although the payments are calculated based on a 20-year repayment schedule, the loan comes due in five. The expiration of the five-year term is called the balloon. The SBA has deemed demand notes and balloon payments to be unreasonable and therefore eligible for refinancing under an SBA program. This is good news for you if you want to take advantage of SBA's favorable terms and conditions.

What types of debt are not eligible for SBA refinancing?

Most types of business loans and leases are eligible to be refinanced under SBA rules, however, there are a couple of exceptions. Loans due to a principal of an applicant's business are ineligible to be refinanced under SBA. If you are an owner of the applicant company and you have loaned it money, you will be unable to be reimbursed for your loan to the company through the SBA loan. SBA will require that this debt be subordinated to the SBA loan. SBA loans also cannot be used to refinance debt originally incurred to finance a purpose that would have been ineligible for SBA financing at the time it was originally made. An example of this is a debt that was incurred to acquire a residential rental property. This debt cannot be refinanced under an SBA loan. Another ineligible use of SBA funds is when the SBA loan is intended to be used to pay a creditor who is in a position to sustain a loss (usually due to business failure) that would cause a shift to SBA of all or part of that potential loss. If the refinance under the new SBA terms and conditions provide reasonable assurance of repayment or additional assets can be acquired so that the new SBA loan becomes fully collateralized, the loan may be eligible. Your SBA loan professional can provide guidance on this issue. If you think your business is going to fail, the lender and

SBA will believe you. If you expect business success and this will be assisted by the SBA loan refinance, the SBA will generally support your request.

To determine if your debt is eligible to be refinanced under an SBA loan program, a business debt schedule should be completed. A sample business debt schedule has been included in Part Five and at www.ApprovedBook.com. Mark each debt that you would like to have your SBA loan professional consider for refinancing with an asterisk (*). Make sure to also include all lease obligations on the debt schedule. It may make sense to consider refinancing these depending on your cash flow. If any of your debts have a hard maturity at which time the balance will not be zero, these debts have balloons which make them eligible for refinancing under SBA so refinancing should be considered.

CHAPTER 5

SBA 7(A) LOAN TERMS AND CONDITIONS

What is the maximum SBA 7(a) loan amount?

SBA loans have a maximum loan amount of $5 million to any one business including affiliates. Consider an affiliate business to be any other business of which any guarantors of the applicant business have at least a 20% ownership interest. For example, if you and I are applying for an SBA loan in which we are 50/50 partners and you also own 25% of another business, the other business will be considered to be an affiliate business. If any of these affiliated businesses have SBA loans outstanding, the outstanding balance is to be subtracted from the $5 million maximum. If you and your partners have multiple SBA loans and you are not exactly sure how this will work for your unique situation, go to www.ApprovedBook.com to access additional information.

What is the maximum dollar amount that will be guarantied by SBA?

The maximum guaranty amount that the SBA allows for you and your affiliated businesses is $3.75 million. This guaranty maximum is relevant to SBA 7(a) loans, SBA Express loans, and various other SBA loan products. Many SBA 7(a) loans are offered with a companion SBA Express loan so the total amount guarantied is calculated by adding all of the guarantied portions of the various SBA loan amounts together. Regardless of the number and type of SBA loans that you have (even if they have been provided by several different SBA lenders), the maximum dollar amount that the SBA will guaranty under the SBA 7(a) and Express program is $3.75 million combined.

What is the guaranty percentage for SBA loans?

For SBA Express loans, the guaranty percentage is 50% of the loan amount. For SBA 7(a) loans up to $150,000, the guaranty percentage is 85% of the loan amount. For SBA 7(a) loans greater than $150,001 up to $5 million, the guaranty percentage is 75% of the loan amount. When the guarantied portion of the SBA Express and SBA 7(a) loans are added, they cannot exceed $3.75 million. For example, if you are offered a $1 million SBA 7(a) loan and a $100,000 SBA Express line of credit, $750,000 of the $1 million SBA 7(a) loan will be guarantied ("insured" by the SBA) and $50,000 of the $100,000 SBA Express line of credit (LOC) will be guarantied ("insured" by the SBA). The total $800,000 is less than $3.75 million, so your request is within the maximum guaranty amount.

How long are the SBA loan terms (maturities)?

SBA 7(a) loans are really popular because their maturities are typically much longer than what is available through conventional (non-SBA) commercial financing. The SBA has set generous term maximums enabling borrowers to repay SBA loans over a longer period of time and with lower monthly payments. Working capital and inventory can be financed over 10 years as well as intangible assets such as goodwill (transferred through a change of ownership). Equipment, fixtures, and furniture can be financed over 10 years and up to 25 years if the lender can document that the economic life of the equipment, fixtures, and furniture each exceeds 10 years. Real estate can be financed over 25 years. If real estate will be constructed or renovated, the construction period may be added to the 25-year maximum maturity.

SBA 7(a) loans that have mixed purposes may use the blended maturity or a maturity up to the maximum for the asset class comprising the largest percentage of use of proceeds. For example, if loan proceeds will be used to purchase $1 million of real estate, $400,000 of inventory, and $100,000 of intangible assets, this would qualify as a loan with mixed purposes. In this case, the SBA lender can choose to use the blended term and finance all $1.5 million over 20 years, or the SBA lender could decide to use the largest percentage of use of proceeds and make the loan payable over 25 years. Most SBA lenders will choose to offer the blended maturity, but you can request the 25-year term to reduce your required minimum monthly loan payments.

What are the typical interest rates for SBA 7(a) loans?

If you are offered an SBA 7(a) loan, it is likely that you will be applying for a loan amount greater than $50,000 and that you will be offered a term that is at least 10 years. The maximum variable interest rate that lenders are allowed to offer you will be the Wall Street Journal (WSJ) Prime Rate plus 2.75%. As of the writing of this book, Wall Street Journal Prime is 3.25%, so 3.25% + 2.75% equates to an interest rate of 6%. Most SBA lenders offer SBA 7(a) loans at WSJ-Prime + 2.75% that will adjust on a quarterly basis. The interest rate will only change if WSJ-Prime changes and the rate is controlled by the Feds. The WSJ-Prime rate has been at 3.25% since December 2008. In some cases, the SBA lender may offer you a fixed rate for a period of time prior to adjusting it or even offer fixed rates for the term of the loan. Fixed rate options are usually only offered for lower-risk transactions substantially secured by commercial real estate. SBA Express loans may be offered at a rate up to WSJ-Prime plus 4.5%.

The interest rates charged for SBA loans may come to you as a surprise. Most SBA applicants have purchased a car and a house prior to applying for a business loan, commercial loan, or SBA loan. Interest rates are determined based on risk. Auto loans are typically the least risky because your car is what gets you to work every day. Your home loan is second because it is the roof over your family. From the lender's perspective, a commercial loan is more risky than a home loan but can be supported by a history of profitability represented on the business's tax returns and financial statements. Commercial loans are also almost always fully secured by commercial real estate. Commercial loan requests not eligible for conventional commercial financing are likewise considered to be even more risky. Credit cards are usually 100% unsecured so are considered to be the most risky and that is why you see rates at 18% or higher. As the risk increases, the interest rate increases. When you have been approved for a loan that is not fully secured (e.g., similar to a credit card but usually with a much larger credit amount), getting a loan priced at 2.75% over Prime should be considered as relatively cheap money. If your SBA loan qualifies for fixed-rate financing, pat yourself on the back and take it.

What are SBA guaranty fees?

SBA guaranty fees are the fees charged by the SBA to provide the SBA loan programs. Without these SBA programs, the 21 advantages discussed in Part One would not exist today. In 2013, over $30 billion in SBA loans were approved to borrowers applying for business credit not available to them through conventional commercial resources. This means that $30 billion in commercial loans would have either not been approved or would have been approved with less favorable terms than the 21 discussed.

The guaranty fees are collected just like insurance premiums to offset the cost of the program including the SBA's guarantied portion of loan defaults. The SBA guaranty to the SBA lender is similar to the liability insurance on your home. If your home were to catch fire, your insurance carrier would pay to rebuild it. Your residential lender requires you to have liability insurance to protect its collateral interest in your home. Similarly, the commercial lender will only give you financing if you get the SBA insurance.

In Part One, we discussed 21 benefits of an SBA loan. The majority of these benefits have to do with terms and conditions of SBA loans that are more advantageous to you than traditional non-SBA loans. Non-SBA loans are made by lenders with terms and conditions that maximize profit to the lender and minimize their risk. SBA loans are offered by these same lenders when the risk is too great for them to offer the loan without the assistance of the SBA. The SBA has enabled lenders to make "riskier" loans because the SBA basically offers them an insurance policy for a percentage of the loan. With any insurance policy, premiums are collected to cover losses. The lender has the opportunity to make more loans generating additional interest income, and the borrower wins with favorable terms.

How is the SBA guaranty fee calculated?

For SBA 7(a) loan amounts of $150,000 or less, the guaranty fee is 2% of the guarantied portion. As you recall, loans up to $150,000 have an SBA guaranty of 85%. If you want to get an SBA 7(a) loan for $100,000, the guarantied portion will be 85% of the loan amount or $85,000. The guaranty fee will be $85,000 times 2% or $1,700 ($100,000 x 85% x 2%).

For SBA 7(a) loan amounts greater than $150,000 and up to $700,000, the guaranty fee is 3% of the guarantied portion. For SBA 7(a) loans over $150,000, 75% of the loan amount is guarantied by the SBA. If you want to get an SBA 7(a) loan for $500,000, the guarantied portion will be $375,000. The guaranty fee will be 3% times $375,000 or $11,250 ($500,000 x 75% x 2%).

For loan amounts greater than $700,000 and up to $5 million, the guaranty fee is a little more complicated. If the guarantied amount is less than $1 million, the guaranty fee is 3.5%. If the guarantied amount is greater than $1 million, the first million dollars has the 3.5% guaranty fee and the fee for the guarantied balance over $1 million is 3.75%. For example, if you have an SBA loan amount of $1 million, the guarantied portion would be $750,000 ($1,000,000 x 75%). In this case the guarantied amount of $750,000 is less than $1 million, so it would be multiplied times 3.5% to result in a guaranty fee of $26,250. If you were to get a $2 million SBA 7(a) loan, the guarantied portion would be $1.5 million ($2,000,000 x 75%). The first million dollars would be multiplied times 3.5%. The $500,000 in excess of the $1 million would be multiplied by 3.75%. The total guaranty fee would be $53,750—(1,000,000 x 3.5%) + (500,000 x 3.75%).

What are the other closing costs?

The SBA guaranty fee is the primary difference between commercial and SBA loans in regard to closing costs. However, to reduce out-of-pocket expenses and make SBA loans more affordable, the SBA has restricted the fees that SBA

differently than loans greater than $350,000. Regardless of the loan size, the cash flow of the SBA applicant is the primary source of repayment, not the liquidation of collateral. Loan amounts of $350,000 or less can be approved through expedited processing.

What is expedited loan processing (loan amounts up to $350,000)?

For loan amounts up to $350,000, the SBA has set up an online system in which SBA loans can be approved based on obtaining a satisfactory SBA credit score. The SBA credit score enables loans to be processed more efficiently than through standard SBA 7(a) processing. The SBA credit score should not be confused with your consumer FICO credit score. The SBA credit score is generated based on a combination of your consumer FICO credit score, your business credit score, business financials, and application data. As of the writing of this book, a consumer FICO credit score of 600 or higher meets this part of the SBA credit score criteria. To establish a business credit score for your company, you will need to get a DUNS number for your company. The minimum SBA credit score is set by SBA and may be adjusted from time to time based on the current SBA portfolio. Loan requests that do not meet the minimum SBA credit score requirements for expedited processing may still be processed under either standard 7(a) processing or under the SBA Express program. Standard 7(a) processing is required for all SBA loans greater than $350,000.

What is a DUNS number and how do I get one?

A DUNS number is a unique nine-digit number to identify your business entity and location. The DUNS number is provided by Dun & Bradstreet, commonly known as D&B. The DUNS number is important for your business to establish business credit. Banks, customers, and suppliers often get D&B information on a company prior to doing business with that company. As of March 27, 2014, the SBA recommends that all SBA borrowers obtain a DUNS number for the purpose of establishing business credit.

To apply for a free DUNS number, go to http://iupdate.dnb.com/iUpdate/companylookup.htm.

On this webpage, click "find your company's DUNS number or request a new DUNS number." You will first search your company by name and location. If your company comes up, select it and request your existing DUNS number. You will fill in your contact information and make sure to select "Federal Government Grantee or Applicant." You will receive your DUNS number by email from govt@dnb.com with subject: Requested DUNS number. If your business and location is not listed, hit the button that says "request a D-U-N-S Number" at the bottom of the page and complete an easy form. You will receive your DUNS number within one to two days by email.

Are there cash flow requirements for loans up to $350,000 (7(a) small loans)?

For SBA loan requests in the amount of $350,000 or less, the SBA requires that the global cash flow of the business must be equal to or greater than a one-to-one coverage ratio on a historical basis or a projected cash flow basis. The SBA also requires that the applicant business have cash flow equal to or greater than a one-to-one coverage ratio on a historical or projected basis. One-to-one coverage means that if a business has "free" cash flow of $100, the business can afford $100 of annual debt payments. For businesses that do not historically have cash flow to support the request, projections can be provided to meet this requirement. Cash flow will be broken down and covered in detail in Part Three.

Are financial statements verified for authenticity?

To verify the authenticity of the tax returns submitted with the application package to the SBA lender, the SBA lender is required to submit the IRS Form 4506-T to the IRS. Tax returns submitted with the request are matched to tax return information filed with the IRS. This protects applicants, the SBA lender, and the SBA from processing fraudulent tax returns. The IRS Form 4506-T will be discussed in the application Part (Part Five). For loan requests supported by financial projections, assumptions supporting the projections are required. How to prepare projections and assumptions will be discussed in the business plan Part (Part Four).

What is standard SBA 7(a) processing?

For SBA loans that are greater than $350,000 or SBA 7(a) loan requests that do not meet expedited processing requirements, standard SBA 7(a) processing is required. SBA loans that are greater than $350,000 require additional credit analysis due to increased risk. The SBA has not set a minimum credit score; however, the cash flow requirements are higher than loans of $350,000 or less. If you are applying for a loan through standard SBA 7(a) processing, the business cash flow must be 1.15 to 1 or greater on a historical and/or projected basis. A 1.15-to-1 coverage ratio means that if a business has free cash flow of $115,000, the business can be approved for up to $100 of annual debt payments. How cash flow is calculated is explained in detail in Part Three. A worksheet to calculate your business's cash flow is available for download at www.ApprovedBook.com.

What is the equity injection (down payment) requirement for SBA loans?

The SBA requires SBA lenders to determine an adequate equity injection for all SBA loan applications. Equity injection typically ranges from 0% to 30%. Most SBA lenders require at least a 10% equity injection for SBA loan requests for the purchase of commercial real estate. It is common for SBA lenders who finance non-franchise start-up businesses occupying leased locations to require up to a 30% equity injection. Start-up businesses occupying leased locations are highly risky from a collateral and cash flow perspective; however, the 30% injection can mitigate the SBA lender's discomfort over the lack of collateral and lack of historical cash flow.

Can your equity injection be borrowed?

Equity injection cannot be borrowed unless you can demonstrate repayment ability of this debt from a source other than the subject business. For example, after submission of your SBA loan application request, you cannot apply for a home equity line of credit for your down payment unless your spouse is going to keep his/her job and has adequate W-2 income from the job to support repayment of the home equity line of credit. Your equity injection can, however, be raised by selling minority shareholder interest in your business to potential investors.

Can non-cash assets be used for equity injection?

Equity injection requirements may be met by providing assets other than cash. A common example of non-cash assets are the fixed assets already on the balance sheet. If the net book value of the assets on the balance sheet or an independent third-party appraisal of the fixed assets is greater than the required equity injection, additional equity injection may not be required. Another example of non-cash equity is "standby debt" in which you get a loan for your down payment; however, repayment of the debt is on full standby meaning that you cannot make any payments towards this debt until the SBA loan is repaid in full. There is wiggle room on this as well, and SBA regularly approves a partial standby period such as two years of no payments followed by principal and interest payments for a specified term. For this to be approved, it must be demonstrated through historical records and/or projected cash flow that the business will be able to support the SBA loan payment and the standby debt payments after the standby period has expired. How this is demonstrated will be discussed in Part Three.

How is equity injection verified by SBA?

Equity injection is a hot button with SBA. SBA and lenders in general have concerns about companies that take on too much debt. A business is more likely to fail if its debt burden is too great. To limit excessive debt burden, SBA lenders are required to determine an adequate cash equity injection and/or reasonable "standby debt" terms for "borrowed injection." For equity injection to qualify as cash equity (non-debt), the SBA requires bank account statements for verification. It is recommended that a business account be opened at the onset of a business loan application and that money be deposited into the account to cover the required equity injection amount plus a reserve of at least $10,000 for any unexpected expenses. The SBA lender is required to document its file with two months of bank statements evidencing that throughout both months, the equity injection was available. Any large transfers in or out of the account during this two-month period should be avoided because those transfers will require additional investigation.

What are the collateral requirements for SBA loans?

As discussed in Part One, an SBA loan cannot be declined solely on the basis of inadequate collateral. The SBA, however, does require that lenders collateralize SBA loans to the maximum extent possible up to the loan amount. The SBA requires that if fixed assets such as commercial real estate and equipment do not fully secure the loan, the lender must take other assets, including available equity in the personal real estate of the principals, as collateral. The SBA considers a loan to be "fully secured" if the lender has taken a security interest in all available fixed assets with a combined "adjusted net book value" equal to the loan amount. "Adjusted" is the liquidation value of an asset set by SBA. "Net book value" (NBV) is defined as an asset's original price minus depreciation and amortization.

What are the collateral requirements for machinery and equipment?

New machinery and equipment will be valued at 75% of the purchase price. This means that if you are purchasing new equipment for $100,000, the lender will calculate that the liquidation value of the equipment is $75,000 (75% of the purchase price). Used machinery and equipment will be valued at 50% of the net book value. Used equipment is likely to have been depreciated on the balance sheet to its net book value. If you are purchasing used machinery and equipment as part of your $100,000 transaction and the balance sheet represents that the equipment has depreciated to $50,000, the lender will calculate that the liquidation value of the equipment is actually only $25,000 (NBV of $50,000 x 50%). If an appraisal is ordered on either new or used machinery and equipment, the liquidation value of the machinery and equipment will be 80% of the appraisal value (i.e., 80% of the appraised value less liens).

Let's imagine that you are purchasing a business for $500,000 to acquire equipment. The seller may have purchased the equipment for $1 million but needs to sell so you have arranged to purchase the operation for $500,000. The seller's balance sheet reports that the equipment was originally purchased for $1 million and that the equipment has been depreciated by $900,000, providing a net book value of $100,000. The SBA lender will recommend that an equipment appraisal be ordered to determine the value. The appraisal comes back indicating that the equipment has a useful life of 25 years and a value of $575,000. Both you and the lender are pleased because the value is not $100,000 but actually $75,000 more than the purchase price. The lender will then calculate that the collateral is worth 80% of this value and credit you with collateral of $460,000 ($575,000 x 80%LTV). If the SBA lender had offered to finance $450,000 of the $500,000 business purchase, the SBA would consider the SBA loan to be fully secured by the equipment and no additional collateral would need to be pledged. As mentioned in Part One, this is a huge advantage over traditional commercial financing as non-SBA lenders would use a 50% LTV (loan to value) versus 80% LTV under SBA rules. In this example, the non-SBA (conventional commercial) financing option would provide you with only $287,500, requiring you to come in with $212,500 to make the exact same purchase.

What are the collateral requirements for real estate?

For SBA loans secured by real estate collateral, 85% of the value of real estate is used as the liquidation value, regardless of the type of real estate. If you want to get an SBA loan to purchase a million-dollar commercial property and the appraisal comes back at the purchase price (for example, $1 million), the lender will credit you for collateral in the amount of $850,000. If the lender has offered you an SBA loan of $900,000, the lender will look for $50,000 of additional collateral (liquidation value) to fully secure the $900,000 loan. To further evidence the benefit of the SBA's 85% rule versus traditional commercial real estate financing, non-SBA loans are traditionally financed for up to 80% LTV for multi-purpose properties, 75% LTV for investment real estate properties, and up to 65% LTV for single purpose (special purpose) properties such as golf courses, car washes, gas stations, and bowling alleys.

Who should order the appraisal?

An appraisal report will be ordered by the SBA lender for all commercial real estate securing a loan of greater than $250,000. Save your money and never personally order commercial real estate appraisals as they must be ordered by the SBA lender and identify the SBA lender as the intended user of the appraisal.

What are the appraisal requirements for construction loans?

For SBA loans that will be used to finance the construction of new commercial real estate or the substantial renovation of an existing building, the appraisal will be prepared on an "as-complete" basis. The appraiser will use the construction plans and specifications and construction contract to prepare an appraisal as if the construction project were already completed. SBA defines "substantial" as rehabilitation expenses of more than one-third of the purchase price or fair market value at the time of the application. If you purchase a building for $1 million, and you will be doing more than approximately $334,000 of construction/renovation, an "as-complete" appraisal will be required. This enables you to get maximum financing based on the value of the completed project.

What if the loan will not be fully secured by real estate, machinery, and equipment?

If available machinery, equipment, and commercial real estate do not fully secure the SBA loan, the SBA lender will next look to the "trading assets" of the business. Trading assets include inventory and accounts receivable. The SBA permits SBA lenders to value trading assets at 10% of the book value represented on the balance sheet. This is a lower value than you might expect. However, the SBA recognizes that when a business is in trouble, trading assets are typically the first to be liquidated in the borrower's attempt to save the business. Under SBA 7(a) loans, trading assets are not closely monitored like they usually are by an asset-based lender or factoring company. The 10% liquidation value is a significant cut; however, in many cases, the 10% of book value can help meet the SBA's definition of fully secured.

When will the SBA require personal property to be pledged as collateral?

If the machinery, equipment, commercial real estate, and trading assets do not satisfy the SBA's collateral requirements, the SBA lender is required to take available equity in the personal real estate of the personal guarantors of the applicant small business. Personal real estate includes personal residences and investment properties. Personal guarantors are the individual owners with at least a 20% interest in the small business applicant. If an individual or an individual and his/her spouse together own 20% or more of the small business applicant, the SBA lender must consider taking as collateral the equity in the personal real estate either owned individually by the applicant owner or available equity in personal real estate owned jointly. If real estate is individually owned by a spouse who has no ownership interest in the applicant business, the non-owner spouse's assets cannot be considered for use as collateral. Assets transferred to the non-owner spouse within six months of application will not be exempt. To insulate non-owner spouses, their assets should be held solely in their individual names.

When will the SBA not require personal property to be pledged as collateral?

Personal real estate is not required by the SBA if the equity in the personal real estate is less than 25% of the property's fair market value. However, SBA lenders have the ability to supersede the SBA and request personal real estate be pledged in these situations. If you have less than 25% equity, negotiate this with the SBA lender during the proposal letter stage. Liens on personal real estate to secure an SBA loan may also be limited to the collateral shortfall. For example, in the above example where the collateral shortfall on the commercial real estate purchase was $50,000, you can request that the lien on your home be only for the $50,000 shortfall versus the entire SBA loan amount, which most lenders would prefer to request. If you own a home worth $200,000 and your home mortgage totals $120,000, you will have $80,000 of equity. Eighty thousand dollars is greater than 25% of your value, so SBA will require that the SBA lender file a lien for at least the collateral shortfall of the SBA loan. In the above example of the $900,000 loan with a $50,000 collateral shortfall, you can request that the SBA lender only file a lien for $50,000, which will be in a junior position to the existing $120,000 residential mortgage amount. If you live in a state where there are tax implications for liens on personal and investment real estate, the lien may be further limited to 150% of the equity in the collateral.

What happens if collateral is not available to fully secure an SBA loan?

Once all available collateral to be taken has been determined in an attempt to fully secure the loan, the SBA lender has satisfied SBA's collateral requirements in the loan approval process. Regardless of whether the loan is deemed to be fully secured, the SBA's eligibility requirements for collateral will be considered to have been met. The collateral taken to secure your SBA loan at the time of loan closing (specified in your collateral agreements) will be the only collateral available to secure the SBA loan for the duration of the loan term.

Is life insurance required for SBA loans?

If an SBA loan is not fully secured, life insurance is required for the principal of sole proprietorships, single member LLCs, and for businesses otherwise dependent on one owner's active participation, consistent with the size and term of the SBA loan. The amount and type of collateral available to repay the loan may be factored into the determination of the appropriate amount of life insurance. If an SBA loan is secured by real estate, the SBA lender will require life insurance for at least the amount of the liquidation collateral shortfall. If you have a million- dollar loan and the liquidation value of the commercial real estate collateral is $850,000, the SBA lender will require a collateral assignment of a life insurance policy of at least $150,000.

Most small businesses fall in the third category in which the success of the business is dependent on the owners. When considering if your business is dependent on your active participation, imagine what would happen to your partners and your family if you were to pass away. Many businesses operated by owners without life insurance policies have left spouses and family members unable to manage their personal lives and business responsibilities. For this reason, the SBA and SBA lenders will require life insurance policies that will pay off the loan balance upon the death of an owner. If the SBA lender determines that a principal is uninsurable, the lender must obtain written verification of uninsurability. The requirement for life insurance may be waived; however, a management succession plan should be put in place and provided to the SBA lender. For a list of life insurance providers that specialize in providing life insurance policies to meet the SBA's requirements, visit www. ApprovedBook.com.

Can SBA loans be used to finance a business acquisition?

SBA loans are commonly used to finance changes of ownership. Business acquisitions (change of ownership) typically involve the sale of both tangible assets such as equipment and inventory and intangible assets such as goodwill. It is unusual to see a situation such as the example discussed (i.e., the purchase of a company for $500,000 with equipment that appraises for $575,000). It is much more common for tangible assets to have an appraised value less than the purchase price with the balance of the purchase price allocated to goodwill. For transactions that involve intangible assets greater than $250,000, the SBA requires SBA lenders to obtain an independent business valuation from a qualified source. If you are acquiring an existing business including the real estate occupied by the existing business, the SBA lender may order a "business enterprise" or "going concern" value appraisal. The going concern appraisal will allocate separate values to the individual components of the transaction, including land, building, equipment, and the business itself (including intangible assets such as goodwill). If real estate is not involved or the SBA lender decides not to order an enterprise appraisal, the lender will order a business valuation performed by another qualified source. This decision will be made based on shortest time for delivery, best price, and the expertise in the area related to the subject business. The business valuation must meet or exceed the amount of the SBA loan allocated for intangible assets. The valuation will also give you comfort that the seller has not overpriced the business.

Can SBA loans be used to finance a franchise business?

Financing a franchise such as Dunkin' Donuts, Subway, or Comfort Inn with an SBA loan is a common practice and very popular. In fact, many SBA lenders prefer financing franchise businesses over non-franchise businesses because systems and procedures have been put into place by franchisors increasing the likelihood for franchisee success. Prior to entering into a franchise agreement, reach out to an SBA professional to find out if the franchise concept that you are interested in financing is eligible for SBA financing. The franchise agreements may need to be reviewed to determine if the agreement imposes unacceptable control provisions held by the franchisor. Affiliation can exist between a franchisor and a franchisee if it is determined that the franchisor has excessive control over the franchisee.

Do SBA loans require personal guaranties?

All SBA loans must be personally guarantied by at least one individual. The SBA requires that all individuals who own 20% or more of the small business applicant must provide an unlimited full personal guaranty. If a spouse owns 5% or greater interest in the small business applicant so that the combined ownership interest of both spouses is 20% or more, spouses with at least 5% ownership also must provide an unlimited full personal guaranty. Non-owner spouses who have joint ownership in personal property pledged as collateral will have to sign on the collateral documents only for their individual interest in the collateral. SBA lenders may require owners of less than 20% ownership to provide limited or unlimited personal guaranties depending on their applicant business responsibilities. In situations where there is no individual who owns 20% or more of the small business applicant, at least one of the owners must provide a full unconditional guaranty. Within six months of application, each owner of 20% or more is required to be a guarantor unless such owner completely divests himself/herself of all ownership interest and severs all relationships with the small business applicant in any capacity, including being an employee, volunteer, or consultant. This six-month lookback period is to prevent owners from trying to avoid the personal guaranty requirement by transferring ownership interest upon discovery that they will have to personally guaranty the loan.

Do SBA loans require corporate guaranties?

All entities such as corporations and LLCs (other than ESOPs) that own 20% or more of a small business applicant must provide an unlimited full guaranty. For trusts owning 20% or more of a small business applicant, the trust must guaranty the loan with the trustee executing the guaranty on behalf of the trust.

If the trust is revocable, the trustor must also provide an unlimited full guaranty. An Employee Stock Ownership Plan (ESOP) may not guaranty a loan regardless of whether it owns 20% or more of a small business applicant. When a 401(k) owns 20% or more of a small business applicant, the owners of the 401(k) must provide their full unconditional personal guaranty regardless of their individual ownership interest in the small business applicant.

What are the other requirements to obtain an SBA loan?

In addition to eligibility, cash flow, equity injection, collateral, and other items discussed in this Part, SBA has specified how SBA lenders are to evaluate you, your partners, your affiliated companies, and the applicant business in their credit analysis. Meeting and exceeding the SBA's and SBA lender's credit profile requirements for loan approval is the focus of Part Three.

PART THREE
YOUR CREDIT PROFILE

This is the section that will teach you everything that no one talks about, but your ability to obtain business financing depends upon it. I'm excited to have this opportunity to show you how you, your business, and your application will be evaluated. This will take a little work on your part but the reward of loan approval will be well worth the time spent understanding how your application will be evaluated. Plus, recommendations throughout this section will enable you to give the SBA lender your most favorable first impression.

Expectations

Your expectations for SBA loan approval are going to range from feeling overly optimistic to overly pessimistic. You may be so confident of loan approval that you expect to be offered better terms than anyone else and immediately upon your request. On the other hand, you may feel that you want to give up because you believe that you have absolutely no chance of getting approved. You may also be feeling overwhelmed. It is time for you to take my hand and let me show you the way.

Unless you originate SBA loans on a daily basis and keep up on all of the regulatory changes, you are not going to be an expert on SBA loan approval. I'm going to take a wild guess that you bought this book to help your chances for obtaining that approval. Congratulations for taking this important step toward that.

As an SBA loan applicant, you are not expected to be an expert in SBA lending, how to complete the SBA application perfectly, nor how to best position yourself, your partners, and your business for loan approval. That is my job. If you want to fix your broken leg, don't come to me, but if you want to position yourself for SBA loan approval, read this book and visit www.ApprovedBook.com throughout the application process.

Knowledge is power and this Part is going to give you all the tools that you need to put SBA loan approval within reach. If you invest the time to really understand how you are going to be evaluated, you will save weeks, months, and even years of frustration.

Introduction

In this section, your credit profile will be discussed in three parts: (1) Your Personal Credit Profile, (2) Your Business Credit Profile and (3) Your Application Credit Profile. Your personal credit profile is all about you, your family, your partners, and your partners' families. We will discuss everything that the SBA lender will evaluate about you, from your personal finances, your professional experience, and life's hurdles that make you who you are. I will also show you how to do the same calculations that the SBA lenders will do to evaluate your personal financial situation. In your business credit profile, I will discuss how an SBA lender will evaluate your business and what SBA lenders see behind the numbers and all the paperwork. I will show you exactly how to look at your business to determine what is good and what is bad from a financing perspective. In the application credit profile, we put it all together: your loan request, your personal profile, and your business profile.

The Five C's of Credit

If you have ever applied for a loan, you have heard of the "Five C's of Credit." You may not know what they are, but I'm sure that you have heard that banks evaluate loans based on this concept. The two most common C's are collateral and cash flow (capacity). Lenders want to know that their loan is both secured by something (collateral) and that there is a source of repayment from the generation of positive cash flow (capacity). Capacity is much more important than collateral. If you have capacity, then you have enough income to cover your loan payments and obligations. From the business perspective, collateral is the least important, other than that it is an asset on the balance sheet. From the lender's perspective, collateral is what it will sell to try to get its money back if you were no longer able to make your loan payments. For most conventional lenders, collateral comes in at number one or number two of importance. The SBA, on the other hand, cares much more about the success of your company than the possible failure of it. For this reason, collateral is listed as number five in importance.

The ideal loan borrower excels in all Five C's of Credit. If you and your business excel in all five categories, then you probably don't need an SBA loan because every conventional lender should be banging on your door to get your business. If no one is doing that, continue reading. Few conventional borrowers excel in all five C's, and for those of you that do excel in all five, the SBA is likely to still be of interest to you now that you have read Part One.

If you are reading this book, your goal is to get financing for your business. Like anything that you want to acquire, you need to know how to get it. Lenders determine if they will give you a loan based on the five C's. I'm not going to bore you with a textbook's worth of information about them, but I am going to give you specific information that you should use to highlight your strengths in each category. I'm also going to show you how to identify and mitigate your weaknesses. This Part is all about showing you how you are going to be evaluated. You and your partners are going to be assessed at the individual level, at the business level, and at the application level. Your application for financing is going to be evaluated from a granular and global perspective. The global perspective is a combination of your family unit, your partners' family units, the applicant business, and your affiliated businesses.

The Five C's of Credit are character, capacity, conditions, capital, and collateral. Character is listed first because it is considered to be the most important of the five C's. Character is determined by an evaluation of reputation, credit history, experience, and other factors to be discussed. Capacity is the measure of a borrower's ability to repay loans by comparing income against debt obligations. Conditions are the factors that have influence over the economic stability of a person and a company. Capital is a borrower's equity investment in a company or toward a project. Capital also includes liquid reserves available for additional investment as needed. Collateral represents assets that are secured by a lender as a secondary source of repayment if the business were to fail. The SBA's goal is to set you up to succeed, so collateral is listed last.

CHAPTER 6

THE PERSONAL CREDIT PROFILE

The personal credit profile is an analysis of the past, present, and projected future of each of the principals of the applicant business. To evaluate your personal credit profile, several pieces of information will be needed including application worksheets discussed in Part Five. The personal credit profile has been divided into five sections to evaluate each of the five C's as they relate to you personally. In this section you will generate a thorough understanding of your personal credit profile from an SBA lender's perspective. Areas identified to be strong should be highlighted and areas identified to be weak should be mitigated. I encourage you to share this information and worksheets with your business partners so that each of them can best highlight their personal strengths and mitigate personal weaknesses. A complete personal profile for each member of your ownership team should be submitted to the SBA lender.

The documents that will be discussed in the personal credit profile section are:

- Personal tax returns (IRS Form 1040, including all schedules)
- Personal financial statement (SBA Form 413)

- Personal income and expense template (download template)
- Management Résumé (download template)
- Statement of Personal History (SBA Form 912)

All template forms can be downloaded from www.ApprovedBook.com.

Personal Character

Personal character is the reputation, experience, and credit history of the individual applicants. The lender is counting on you personally to use the money borrowed to benefit your business and to repay the loan as mutually agreed. Regardless of the strength of the other four C's of credit—i.e., capacity (cash flow), conditions, capital, and collateral—the business is unlikely to repay the loan without you and your personal commitment.

To determine personal character, we are going to discuss your résumé, your credit report, the SBA Form 912, and your public profile. Character is a reflection of who you are as a person and the impression of competence that you portray. During the loan application process, the lender only has a short period of time to determine your character. It is critical that you present yourself in your best light. If you are applying for an SBA loan, in effect you are applying to be hired by the SBA lender and SBA for the CEO position of a company for a term of up to 25 years. Are you going to meet the qualifications of someone who will successfully manage the business? Will you do whatever it takes to make sure that your loan is repaid as agreed? Does your résumé represent your ability to be the CEO of the applicant company? What does your past say about you? I'm going to show you exactly what you should do to shine for personal character.

Résumé

Your résumé will be one of the first items that an SBA lender will flip to when evaluating your personal character. The résumé speaks to your experience relative to managing and running a business. An SBA résumé such as the one available at www.ApprovedBook.com should be completed. Instructions as to how to complete the SBA résumé correctly are detailed in Part Five. Time spent on your résumé is well worth the effort. Too many applications are submitted with insufficient résumé information, giving the lender the impression that the applicant doesn't have the experience to run the applicant business. Don't make that mistake. The first page of the résumé template in Part Five is for general information about your experience and character. The second page of the résumé is where you have the opportunity to detail all of your transferable experience as it relates to the applicant business. The SBA lender must be able to justify your ability to effectively operate and manage the applicant business.

In the work experience section, make sure to provide information from a management perspective. If you have had a sophisticated management title that people outside of your field would not understand, list something more generic like "department manager" for the title and then detail what management rolls and duties you performed in the responsibilities section. Do not expect your lender to be an expert in your area of business expertise. List your title and responsibilities in a way that a high school student would understand what you do.

The amount of education required to run a business ranges from none to having a PhD. Some businesses can be managed by owners without any credentials while others require special designations, licenses, or certificates. Make sure to list at least the highest level of education that you received. Depending on the business for which you are requesting funding, your education will be considered.

If you or any of your partners has ever filed for personal or corporate bankruptcy protection, details surrounding the bankruptcy will be required. The loan officer will need to be able to justify that the circumstances causing you to file were beyond your control. The loan officer will also need to justify your credit history and character to show that the bankruptcy was an anomaly and that you are not likely to go down that path again. For SBA purposes, this justification can only be made if federal debt was not included in the bankruptcy. Anyone who is delinquent on a federal debt or disbarred from doing business with the US government is ineligible for SBA financing.

Did you know that Internet gambling is a source of revenue for human trafficking and other illegal activity? If you do not gamble over the Internet or the games that you play are free, check "no" to questions about this. If you have ever applied for credit in another name such as Phil instead of Philip, check "yes" and list your alternate names. This helps SBA lenders verify information on your credit report and background checks. If you are currently delinquent for business or personal taxes, to obtain SBA financing you must have a written agreement with the tax authority for repayment. Any government debts that are presently delinquent longer than 90 days must be brought current prior to applying for additional government financing such as an SBA loan.

Credit Report

Prior to applying for SBA financing or any type of financing, it is important that you know what is on your credit report. You can access your report from any of the top three credit bureaus (i.e., Experian, TransUnion, or Equifax) or at a site such as annualcreditreport.com. Some lenders judge your character simply on your credit score, so maintaining good credit is important. Correcting errors is also important. Prior to applying for any type of credit, you should order a credit report and print it in its entirety. There is no minimum credit score to qualify for SBA lending, however, the SBA does require a written explanation for delinquencies. A few 30-day late accounts several months back is OK to the SBA, but an explanation needs to be provided in writing. All of us have misplaced or never received an invoice, so a 30-day delinquency happens. Not providing any explanation will give the SBA and the SBA lender the impression that you don't care about the delinquency or the creditor. A common opinion in the lending world is that if an applicant doesn't care enough to repay one creditor's loan, the applicant is unlikely to repay another, so lending to that person is not worth the risk.

After you print off your credit report, go through it line by line. Look at each of your accounts to make sure that you are familiar with them. Collection accounts commonly show up for debts that you may not even be aware of or that you paid off. For SBA loan purposes, it's in your best interest to call the collection company and request a letter stating that you have a zero balance. If you have a collection balance, pay the balance and request that a letter be immediately sent to your fax or email address. You want these letters to prove that balances have been paid in full. Be ahead of the game. The SBA lender will request these letters and you also want the written evidence to make sure the credit report agencies remove it from your credit report. If any of your accounts indicate derogatory payment history such as delinquencies of 30, 60, 90, or 120 days, failed to pay, or anything other than OK, call the creditor if you're not sure why it's listed. Write the explanation for the delinquency next to the account listed on your credit report. If any of your accounts are currently delinquent, immediately call the creditor or log in online and bring the account current.

Do not close any credit card accounts, especially those that currently have a balance. If you have credit cards with a balance that you want to pay off permanently, cut them up and then work to pay them off. Calling a creditor to close an account with a balance due will immediately drop your credit score as you will in effect be terminating a relationship with a creditor to which you still owe money. Keeping your accounts open regardless of balance is important to represent a long credit history. If you have credit card balances in excess of 16% of your limit, do your best to pay them down below 16%. Make sure that none of your credit card balances are in excess of 90%.

Once you have brought any delinquent debt current and reduced credit card balances, print off a statement to reflect the corrected information. Also print all letters received from collection agencies to document satisfied collection debts. In addition, prepare a document listing all accounts that had derogatory information. List the account name (creditor), the account number, the dates of delinquencies, and your explanation. Do this for each of the accounts with derogatory information and then at the bottom of the page make a statement to the effect that all of your debt is current, you are a responsible borrower, and your payments going forward will always be made as agreed. The best loan applicants have no derogatory credit history, indicating to the lender that they are responsible with their debts and will be a low risk for additional borrowing. For loan applicants without perfect credit, providing lenders with written explanation of any derogatory information at the time of application will reflect that you had a bump in the road but that you are responsible and unlikely to default again. To download a sample credit report explanation letter, visit www.ApprovedBook.com. Save all of this information with a copy of your current credit report.

Public Profile

During the underwriting process and usually prior to submission of your application to underwriting, your name and aliases will be searched to learn about your public and private profile. Variations of your name will be searched publicly through common search engines such as Google, Yahoo, Ask, and Bing. Other websites that may be searched include spokeo.com, whitepages.com, dogpile. com, clusty.com, zabasearch.com, zoominfo.com, pipl.com, intelius.com, and anywho.com. Your name may also be searched on Facebook, Twitter, LinkedIn, and other social media sites to determine how you represent yourself publicly. Representations that you have made in the application are easily verified online. County and state public records will also be searched for arrests, lawsuits, liens, and other information.

Prior to applying for any type of loan or employment opportunity, make sure to check what Google says about you. Also, update your Facebook, LinkedIn, and other social media sites to reflect a profile that best represents you as you would like to be perceived.

Prior Loss to the US Government

The character issue most scrutinized by the SBA and the US government is your history of loan default on government-backed loans. If you have defaulted on a loan provided or guarantied by the government and the government took a loss, you are ineligible to receive any other government loans until the debt is repaid in full. As discussed in Part One, government loans are issued to borrowers under terms that are more favorable than those which borrowers can obtain from other financing sources. These loans typically enable you to do something that no other loan source is willing to provide without the government's assistance. Recipients of these loans should consider themselves privileged because they are offered despite the risk. Additional risk requires additional fees to offset the risk. To help keep fees to a minimum, once again, individuals who have defaulted on government loans creating a loss are ineligible to participate in any government loan program again until their debt in default has been repaid. It's a tough rule but makes sense for the public at large who have repaid their government loans and benefited from relatively inexpensive government assistance programs.

Several of the application forms completed during the application process will ask if you have ever defaulted on a federal loan or federally assisted financing resulting in a loss to the government. Common government loans include FHA home mortgages and federal student loans. However, this rule does not apply to conventional home mortgage loans that were later sold to government affiliates such as Fannie Mae or Freddie Mac.

Statement of Personal History (SBA Form 912)

At the time of application, you will complete the SBA Form 912 (and/or SBA Form 1919) that will ask about your arrest history. If you are presently subject to an indictment, charged with a crime, currently on parole or on probation, you are not eligible for SBA financing. If you have been arrested in the last six months, a criminal background check will have to be processed prior to SBA loan approval. If you have ever been convicted, pled guilty, or been placed on any form of parole or probation, a criminal background check will have to be processed prior to SBA loan approval.

If you or any of your partners (including key management) are subject to a criminal background check, immediately inform your SBA loan officer so the processing may begin. Criminal background checks can take as long as 60 to 90 days; however, this can be processed at the same time other application and underwriting procedures are being performed, which can reduce some of this delay. For detailed instruction for how to complete the Statement of Personal History form (SBA Form 912) correctly to avoid delays, see Part Five.

Personal Capacity

Personal capacity is a family's ability to generate adequate income to support the family's expenses and lifestyle. To determine personal capacity, we are going to discuss your personal financial statement, your personal income and expense template, your credit report, your lifestyle, and your sources of income. To get the most from this section, complete a personal financial statement and personal income and expense template. Both of these forms can be downloaded from www.ApprovedBook.com. How to complete these forms accurately is detailed in Part Five.

When considering a business loan application, be prepared for the loan officer to probe into your personal life, including asking several questions about your personal lifestyle. This includes what cars you drive, your sources and income level, how many homes you have, your retirement and investment accounts, if and when your kids are going to college, pending lawsuits, cash in the bank, etc. The reason for this is that the banker has to determine a business owner salary for you (for underwriting purposes only) that is adequate to support your lifestyle. This salary amount generated for underwriting purposes is not to be confused with a banking requirement of what your actual income should or should not be.

In this section, I will show you how your owner salary is generally calculated. Every bank (and finance company) calculates owner's salary slightly differently; however, the steps that I am going to walk you through will eliminate much of the discrepancies between what you actually need for your owner salary and what the lender will calculate you need. To be conservative, a lender will always calculate that you need a larger salary than you may actually require. This sounds good, but actually the higher the calculated owner salary, the less money the business will have available to pay the loan. The result is that the lender may offer a much lower loan amount than you may be entitled to.

Debt-to-Income Ratio (DTI)

A common term in the mortgage industry is debt-to-income or DTI. This takes into account all of your monthly obligations reported on your personal credit report. For example, let's say that John and Mary Adams have decided to purchase a business of which they will share 100% ownership. The banker pulls their credit and sees that John has a car loan for $500/month, that Mary has a car loan for $450/month, they have a home mortgage of $2,500/month, and monthly credit card payments of $300/month. The banker confirms that these are the only personal debt obligations, adds them up, and determines that John and Mary have monthly debt obligations of $3,750 ($500 + $450 + $2,500 + $300 = $3,750/month) or $45,000/year.

So, Mary and John need $45,000 to pay their monthly debt obligations; however, this doesn't take into account their taxes (income, real estate, etc.), insurance, food, gas, utilities, childcare, vacations, and other personal expenditures. To account for this, many lenders consider that debt obligations typically make up 45% of gross income. The bank will now divide John and Mary's annual debt obligations ($45,000) by 45% and determine that John and Mary need an "officer salary" of $100,000.

As an alternative to the 45% DTI calculation, some lenders offer applicants the option to complete a personal income and expense template. The personal income and expense analysis takes into account all of a borrower's personal income and expenses. For households with minimal non-debt obligations, the resulting "officer salary" requirement will be lower.

From the lender's perspective, lenders want to see that the officer salary is not going to be a hardship for the business to support. Bankers generally want to see that the business has the capacity to support 125% of the proposed loan amount after the officer salary deduction. Let's assume that a business broker has determined that the cash flow available for debt service is $300,000. In our example, Mary and John need $100,000 to support their personal lifestyle, so $100,000 is deducted, leaving $200,000 for debt service.

To determine the maximum loan that this business could support, the lender will work backwards from the $200,000 available for debt service. The $200,000 will be divided by 1.25% to determine a 25% cash flow cushion for ups and downs in the business, resulting in $160,000. The banker will next divide the $160,000 by 12 months to determine that the maximum monthly payment that the business can support is $13,333/month. Using a 6% interest rate and a typical 10-year term for business acquisition financing, the banker will determine that John and Mary's business can support a loan of $1.2 million.

Based on an officer salary requirement of $100,000 in this example, the business supports a loan of $1.2 million. If the personal lifestyle (personal capacity calculation) was not $100,000 but instead $50,000 due to different circumstances, the business cash flow would support a loan of $1.5 million or $300,000 more.

Business applicants with lower lifestyle requirements are more easily financed than those with more extravagant lifestyles. If possible, it is recommended that personal debt obligations be eliminated or refinanced to better terms prior to requesting business financing.

Also, if there are other sources of income such as a spouse's income that will continue following acquisition of the business, these will help mitigate financial burdens that the new owners will have on the business. For example, if Mary will be keeping her job that pays her $75,000 per year, the business would actually only need to provide an officer salary of $25,000 versus $100,000, supporting a loan of $1.65 million.

Personal Financial Statement (SBA Form 413)

The first step to calculate personal capacity is to complete a personal financial statement. If the SBA Form 413 (personal financial statement) does not provide you with enough space to detail all of your personal assets and liabilities, download the PFS Addendum from www.ApprovedBook.com. The addendum collects all of the information requested on the SBA Form 413 but in a format that can accept a much larger quantity of information. The totals generated on the addendum can then be simply transferred to the SBA Form 413.

When completing your personal financial statement, make sure to only include assets that are personally owned and liabilities that are personally owed. If any assets are not owned in your (or your spouse's) personal name, do not list them on your personal financial statement in the assets section. If any of your liabilities (car loans, mortgage loans, credit cards, etc.) are paid by your businesses (not personally), do not list them on your personal financial statement in the liabilities section. All assets and liabilities owned and paid by businesses will be accounted for in the business credit profile section. You do not want the lender to double-count your assets and liabilities, first on the personal side and then again on the business side. Make sure that you have accounted for all personal liabilities listed on your personal credit report. For detailed instructions on how to complete the personal financial statement on a line-by-line basis, see Part Five.

Personal Income and Expense Form

The second step to calculate personal capacity is to complete the personal income and expense template. You can download this form from www.ApprovedBook. com. To complete this form, you will need your most recent personal tax return

(IRS Form 1040), your personal financial statement (SBA Form 413), and access to current bill statements.

The personal income and expense template is your opportunity to tell the lender exactly how much income you currently generate as well as what you project to generate after obtaining the SBA loan. The expense portion of the worksheet is where you will detail all of your current personal living expenses. These expenses cover everything on your credit report and everything your family spends money on that is not on your credit report, such as food, clothing, utilities, cable, and taxes. The expense portion of the income and expense worksheet is more important than the income portion because this tells the lender exactly how much income you need to earn to afford your lifestyle. It is easier to finance an owner with minimal personal expenses than an owner with tons of debt and an extravagant lifestyle. What you list as your current expenses will be used to calculate your personal income requirement. If your projected personal income (without income from the applicant business) after obtaining the SBA loan offsets some or all of your personal expenses, your personal income requirements drawn from the applicant business will be less. For example, if your W-2 income will go away because you are going to quit your job to run the applicant business but your spouse will continue working, your spouse's W-2 income will be listed under projected income.

If you do not provide a personal income and expense template, the lender and SBA will be forced to guess what your noncredit report expenses are and lenders will estimate on the high side. For instance, if your monthly obligations reported on your credit report are $5,000 per month, the lender will more than double this amount to estimate your income needs. As previously noted, most lenders assume that your credit report debt represents between 40% and 50% of your income. Five thousand dollars per month in debt reported on your credit report can indicate that you need monthly income of $12,500. This is an annual salary of $150,000 to support $60,000 of annual debt payments, leaving $90,000 to support your noncredit report personal lifestyle and taxes. It sounds absurd; however, this is common practice in all types of commercial and residential lending. If your actual household expenses, including taxes and insurance, are only $3,000, your total monthly expenses would be $8,000, not $12,500. You and the lender share the same interest in having a high salary; however, from the lender's perspective, there is a big difference between having a high salary versus *needing* a high salary to support your lifestyle. Do your best to limit the amount that you list for your personal expenses without coming up with a personal expense budget that is unrealistic for you to live within.

If you haven't completed your personal financial statement and personal income and expense template, do so now. Forms can be downloaded from www.ApprovedBook.com. Instructions for how to complete each form correctly are detailed line by line in Part Five.

Personal Credit Report

In the personal character section, you may have downloaded a copy of your credit report. We are now going to cover how the information on that report impacts your personal capacity. After you print off the report, go through all of your liabilities and make notes about what the various accounts are for, such as "John's car," "primary residence," and "rental property at 123 Main Street." Some of your credit cards may be listed under a name that is not familiar to you. This is because most retail stores that offer you a 10% discount when you opened the card actually issue the card through a third-party finance company or bank. If you are not sure about any accounts, match up account numbers or the monthly payment amount with the statements that you receive in the mail or online. If any of the debts listed on your personal credit report are paid by a business or third party such as a relative for whom you cosigned on the liability, make note of this on the report. The greater the detail, the less questions you will be asked and the faster your loan will be approved. Make sure that all liabilities that are listed on your personal credit report and that are paid personally (by you or your spouse) are listed on your personal financial statement. If real estate taxes and insurance are collected as part of your monthly mortgage payment, note this as well and make note of this on the personal income and expense template in the comments section.

Personal Tax Return (1040)

Your personal tax returns and supporting documentation such as W-2s will be used by the lender to verify your various sources of income and tax liabilities. Your personal tax return will also indicate to the lender your ownership interests in affiliate companies from which additional income can be generated. Affiliate businesses can also be a source of personal liability if the affiliated businesses show a loss and require a capital infusion by you.

Discrepancies between your most recently filed personal tax return and your current personal financial statement and current personal income and expense template can be justified through current payroll checks, W-2s, or other documentation. If you have filed an amended personal tax return, be sure to indicate this to your SBA loan officer and turn in all versions of your filed personal tax returns. Tax returns submitted to the SBA lender are verified for authenticity by comparing your paper tax returns to tax transcripts provided by the IRS.

Ownership in Other Businesses

Many entrepreneurs and business loan applicants have sources of income in addition to their spouse's income and income from investments. Many entrepreneurs have income from ownership in various other businesses. If you own any business other than the applicant business, the profitability of that business will be included in the calculation of your personal capacity. For SBA purposes, consider all "other businesses" to be businesses of which you have at least a 20% ownership interest. SBA considers these other businesses to be "affiliate businesses." You should prepare a simple cash flow analysis for each of them. The affiliate business cash flow calculation will be discussed in detail in the Business Capacity section. See affiliate business capacity in Part Two: Business Capacity.

Personal Capacity Analysis

After completing your personal financial statement and personal income and expense template (following instructions in Part Five), you will have exactly what the lender needs to analyze your personal capacity. If your projected income (without any income from the applicant business) is greater than your personal expenses, your personal capacity will be positive. If your projected income (without any income from the applicant business) is less than your personal expenses, your personal capacity will be negative. Positive capacity is excellent, however, negative personal capacity is common and OK. Negative personal capacity means that you need to draw money from the applicant business and/or from other sources to support your personal lifestyle. Lenders realize that the whole purpose of you owning the applicant business is to generate additional income for yourself and your family, however, they have to calculate whether your lifestyle can be supported by the business without creating financial stress.

The dollar amount listed in the bottom right corner of the personal income and expense template will be used in the application capacity section of Part Three.

Personal Conditions

Personal conditions are the life events that have an influence over your livelihood and lifestyle. These are the circumstances that come up that you may or may not be expecting. Examples of personal conditions include births, deaths, illnesses, weddings, divorces, college tuitions, promotions, raises, demotions, job losses, inheritances, lawsuits, car accidents, obligations, family support, weather, time availability, vacations, drug addictions, gambling problems, SBA eligibility, and many more. To determine your personal conditions, we are going to discuss eligibility, business ownership interests, and potential future events that may impact your *personal conditions*.

At the bottom of page one of the résumé template described in Part Five and available at www.ApprovedBook.com, there are several questions that are asked to determine your personal conditions profile. A common condition that results in loan decline has to do with pending lawsuits. If you or any of your affiliated businesses are involved in a pending lawsuit at the time of application, you will want to detail on a separate sheet of paper the circumstances of the lawsuit and the implications that the lawsuit will have on your ability to run the business. Lawsuits are a red flag and tend to lead to loan denial if the lender believes the lawsuit could at a minimum bring you or your business bad press. If you are in any lawsuit other than an insurance claim, such as for a minor car accident, make sure to detail why the lawsuit will not impact you and your business. If there is any way that you can terminate a lawsuit prior to applying for a commercial or SBA loan, it is recommended. Pending and prior lawsuits are easy to find on the Internet and loan officers want to be able to represent to the approval committee that you have none pending.

To score well for personal conditions when applying for a loan, you want to come across as stable, organized, and predictable. Ideally, your finances are in order and your kids' college tuition has been funded through 529 plans. You should have a variety of insurance policies, including health, life, and property insurance. You don't sue people, have never been sued, and your family gets along like the Brady Bunch.

Life events happen and small fluctuations to your finances are expected. How you handle the conditions of your life may impact the lender's opinion of you. Do your best to keep your life in order, at least during the underwriting process. Also do your best to be positive and responsive to your loan officer's questions, requests for information, and sometimes duplicate requests for information. Some of the most promising loan applications are declined or abandoned because a lender becomes uncomfortable with a borrower based on delays, communication challenges, and borrower frustrations.

Personal Capital

Personal capital is an analysis of your personal sources of working capital. From the lender's perspective, liquid assets versus debt are the best sources of personal working capital. Liquid assets include cash, marketable securities such as stocks and bonds, and cash surrender value of life insurance. Personal working capital can be invested as your equity contribution in a business. Most SBA lenders require at least a 10% equity injection toward a financed project. Personal capital is a common source for this equity injection. Personal capital is also a source of ongoing capital for a business without other sources of capital during times that business expenses are greater than the business's income.

To determine your personal capital, we are going to discuss your personal financial statement. Lenders consider the personal financial statement to be the primary source of information to evaluate personal capital. Each of the individual owners who are expected to invest toward the project or personally guaranty the applicant business will be evaluated for personal capital based on their personal financial statement. To download a personal financial statement template, visit www.ApprovedBook.com. For detailed instruction as to how to correctly complete the personal financial statement, go to Part Five.

Sources of capital listed on your personal financial statement include cash, checking accounts, savings accounts, CDs, money market accounts, retirement accounts, personal accounts/notes receivable, cash surrender value of life insurance policies, stocks, bonds, home equity lines of credit, credit cards, and personal lines of credit. Other sources of capital include the sale of personal assets and gifts. Personal assets such as cars, furniture, equipment, and personal collections can be sold and converted to cash. Receiving gifts from family and friends is also a common source of capital when they want to help you with your business with no strings attached (no required repayment).

Any money previously invested from your personal resources should be communicated to the lender. It's common for entrepreneurs to get excited about a new project and start buying "stuff" such as equipment before a loan application has been approved. At the time of application, your SBA lender should tell you to freeze (to the extent possible) your project spending until underwriting has been completed. This enables the lender to catch up and document everything properly and eliminate a moving application. The SBA lender (and you) wants to credit you for every dollar that you have personally invested toward a project. Thousands of dollars of previously invested capital can be missed during the application process due to communication failures and documentation failure between applicant and lender. This includes hard costs such as land or equipment and soft costs such as architect fees and other professional fees.

Prior to applying for business credit (business loans), many entrepreneurs look to personal sources of capital. Next to liquid assets such as cash, home equity lines of credit are usually the cheapest source of capital for a small business. Money borrowed by you on your home equity line of credit may then be loaned by you to your business. It is also common for people to turn to debt as their primary source of capital. For instance, if you want to purchase a new couch, you may pay for it with your credit card or a new store credit card. While this credit card is a source of (working) capital, it may not be your best from a lender's perspective. Do your best to rein in your spending (and using debt such as credit cards) prior to submitting a loan application. If you have more than $10,000 in credit card debt, the lender is going to question if you live beyond your income level, representing financial irresponsibility. If you can afford to pay off credit card debt without impacting the cash reserved for the application, do so unless there are special circumstances such as a special interest rate.

Personal Collateral

Personal collateral is all of the collateral that is personally owned by the individual applicants that could be considered as collateral to secure an SBA loan. To determine your personal collateral, we are going to discuss your personal financial statement.

Almost every asset listed on your personal financial statement can be used as a source of collateral to secure loans. However, SBA is picky and picky to your benefit. Cash and marketable securities are a great source of collateral and can be loaned against for up to 100% of their value. Your personal cars and trucks can also serve as collateral for financing. While in the past personal vehicles were commonly used to secure SBA loans, these are typically no longer used to collateralize these loans.

Personal real estate, including investment properties, is an excellent source of collateral to help secure SBA loans. In cases where the assets of the business do not fully secure the loan, the SBA loan officer and/or SBA are required to consider real estate assets on your personal financial statement. They will be looking for equity in real estate, which is the difference between the market value of the real estate and the mortgages and lines of credit against it. Make sure to indicate on your personal financial statement all types of liens against your real estate properties. If you happen to have a zero balance on an open home equity line of credit, the actual equity available for an additional lien to the SBA lender will be much less than it appears. This is because at any time, you could use the line of credit up to the credit limit, which sometimes eliminates all of your equity. Make sure to indicate the limit on the home equity line of credit as well as the current balance on your personal financial statement.

If the equity in your personal real estate is less than 25% of its value, the SBA does not require the real estate to be pledged as collateral; however, SBA lenders are allowed to supersede the SBA and require a lien on the collateral. If the equity is less than 25%, you may be able to negotiate out of this lien. In situations where the real estate is owned solely by a spouse who is not an owner of the business, this real estate cannot be required to collateralize the SBA loan. For additional information about collateral, see Part Two.

CHAPTER 7

THE BUSINESS CREDIT PROFILE

The business credit profile is an analysis of the past, present, and projected future of the applicant business. To evaluate your business credit profile, several pieces of information will be required, including application worksheets discussed in Part Five. The business credit profile has been broken into five sections to evaluate business character, business capacity, business conditions, business capital, and business collateral. In this section you will generate a thorough understanding of your business credit profile from the SBA lender's perspective. Areas identified to be strong should be highlighted, and areas identified to be weak should be mitigated.

The documents that will be discussed in the business credit profile section include:

- Business tax returns
- Profit and Loss Statement (income statement)
- Balance Sheet
- Business Debt Schedule (download template)

- Schedule of Collateral (download template)
- Accounts Receivable Schedule (A/R)
- Accounts Payable Schedule (A/P)
- Business Plan (download template—Business Plan Questionnaire)
- Financial Projections (download template)
- Business Capacity Calculator (download template)
- Company contracts and agreements

All template forms can be downloaded from www.ApprovedBook.com.

Business Character

Business character is the reputation, experience, and credit history of the applicant business.

Much of the reputation, experience, and credit history is dependent on the leadership and key employees of the company. To determine business character, we are going to discuss the key management positions, the business's credit report, and the business's public profile.

Key Management Positions and Responsibilities

Without getting overly technical, the SBA and SBA lender need to understand the roles and responsibilities of the owners and staff at the company. Much of this information can be obtained from the business plan, company website, business information application form, and from completing application templates available at www.ApprovedBook.com. It is critical for the SBA to understand the roles and responsibilities of the owners and employees of a company. Companies have a higher probability of success when roles and responsibilities are well defined. This also simplifies and reduces interruptions during changes of ownership and personnel.

Business Credit Report

All SBA lenders are required to obtain a business credit report on the applicant business. The SBA will pull a credit report for the applicant business from Dun & Bradstreet (D&B). To encourage businesses to establish business credit, the

SBA highly recommends all business applicants obtain a DUNS number, which, as mentioned previously, is the unique nine-digit number that identifies your business. Establishing business credit can catapult your business's ability to obtain financing and compete on an international basis with far less reliance on the individual owners. If your business currently does not have a DUNS number, you can get a free one by going to https://fedgov.dnb.com/webform. Additional information about a DUNS number is available in Part Two.

At this time, your business credit reports may provide limited information about your business's lines of credit and loans; however, establishing credit takes time. Business credit reports are good at identifying lawsuits, judgments, and liens. If you are aware of any lawsuits or judgments, provide any details to your loan officer, including potential financial burdens to the business. Lawsuits and judgments are a red flag to lenders, however many are covered by your insurance or can be mitigated by providing evidence of their insignificance and/ or resolution prior to loan closing.

Public Profile

Just like when you're being assessed on your personal character, during the underwriting process and usually prior to submission of your application to underwriting, the applicant business and affiliated trade names will be researched to learn about the company from a public perspective. The business name will be searched publicly through common search engines such as Google, Yahoo, Ask, and Bing. The business's various websites will also be searched. Lenders will also order Dun & Bradstreet (or other) searches as well as county and state lien searches. Information about the applicant small business can be found at the Better Business Bureau, manta.com, spokeo.com, whitepages.com, dogpile.com, zabasearch.com, zoominfo.com, pipl.com, intelius.com, anywho.com, and more. Your business name may also be searched on Facebook, Twitter, LinkedIn, and other social media sites to determine how the business is represented publicly.

The point is that representations that you make in the application are easily verified online. County and state public records will also be searched for judgments, lawsuits, and liens. Prior to applying for any type of business loan, make sure to check what Google says about the company and update the company's Facebook, LinkedIn, and other social media sites if the information is dated or inaccurate.

A benefit of having a good website is that SBA and your SBA loan officer can quickly get lots of information about your company without asking you a ton of questions. A good public presence reflects positively for business character. If you do not have a website, that is fine; however, it should be something to put on the "to-do list."

Business Capacity

Business capacity is a business's ability to generate cash flow in excess of its liabilities. To determine business capacity, we are going to discuss the business debt schedule, the balance sheet, and the profit and loss statement.

Business Cash Flow

The first step in determining business capacity is determining how much cash flow a business generates. Gross cash flow is cash flow before repaying business debt. For SBA loan purposes, gross cash flow is defined as earnings before interest, taxes, depreciation, and interest, otherwise known as EBITDA. EBITDA in its most basic form is net income (NI) plus interest (I) plus depreciation (D) plus amortization (A). The gross cash flow formula is EBITDA = NI + I + D + A. Net Income (NI) is the same thing as Earnings Before Taxes (EBT).

To compute EBITDA without looking all over the business tax return, flip to the income statement page of the return. If the business is an S Corporation, you will look for a page that has "Form 1120S" printed in the top left. If the business is a C Corporation, you will look for a page that has "Form 1120" printed in the top left. If the business is a partnership (LLC or LP), you will look for a page that has "Form 1065" printed in the top left. If the business is reported on a personal tax return, you will look for a page that has "Schedule C (Form 1040)" printed in the top left. If you do not have a tax return but have company prepared financial statements, you are going to look for the form that says "Profit and Loss" or "Income Statement" at the top of the page. All of these forms will provide the same basic information. Income will be reported first, expenses will be reported second, and the net profit or net loss will be reported at the bottom.

Instructions for calculating EBITDA are detailed below based on whether you are looking at Form 1120S, Form 1120, Form 1065, Schedule C of Form 1040, or a profit and loss statement (income statement). There may be circumstances when the amounts shown on the income statement page may be further adjusted by the lender to calculate cash flow; however, if business financials require additional adjustments from EBITDA, the SBA lender will discuss this with you directly. No business is exactly the same; however, SBA has defined EBITDA to be the foundation of how gross cash flow is to be calculated. To simply calculate the cash flow of your business, download a business capacity calculator from www.ApprovedBook.com.

Business Cash Flow—Form 1120S (S Corporation)

On the Form 1120S, you are going to look for the amount listed next to the line item, "Ordinary Business Income (Loss)." On the 2013 Form 1120S, this is line 21. Circle or highlight this dollar amount. This dollar amount is the business's net income (NI), and it may be negative or positive. Next you are going to look for the interest expense. On the 2013 Form 1120S, this is line 13. Highlight or circle this dollar amount. This dollar amount will represent the business's interest expense (I) paid for existing financing. The interest expense may be zero. You are now going to look for the depreciation amount. Depreciation is line 14 on the 2013 Form 1120S. Highlight or circle the amount listed next to line 14. The depreciation amount may be zero.

You have now found the "NI" (EBT), the "I," and the "D" of the EBITDA formula. Amortization will be included in the "other deductions" row. If there is a dollar amount listed next to "other deductions" (line 19 of the 2013 Form 1120S), you will need to flip through the rest of the tax return to find the schedule where the "other deductions" will be broken out. Other deductions are typically located near the back of the tax return. If amortization is not listed as an expense, amortization is zero. If it is listed, highlight or circle the dollar amount.

You now have all of the components to compute EBITDA for a business filed on the 1120S. Add "NI" plus "I" plus "D" plus "A," and you will have computed the business's cash flow. If this business is currently leasing its business space from a landlord (paying rent) and the loan request is to purchase or construct a building in which the business will no longer pay rent to a landlord but instead will be making a mortgage payment, you can change EBITDA to EBITDAR. Only in this case, circle or highlight this amount listed next to "rent" (line 11 of the 2013 Form 1120S) and add the rent (R) amount to EBITDA to calculate cash flow based on EBITDAR. If you will be acquiring this business and you are not currently an owner, you can change EBITDA to EBITDAS. The "S" represents the seller's salary. On IRS Form 1120S, the seller's salary is listed next to "compensation of officers" (line 7 on the 2013 Form 1120S). Only in this case, circle or highlight this amount listed next to "compensation of officers" and add the seller's salary (S) amount to EBITDA to calculate cash flow based on EBITDAS.

Business Cash Flow—Form 1120 (C Corporation)

On the Form 1120, you are going to look for the amount listed next to the line item "taxable income before net operating loss deduction." On the 2013 Form 1120, this is line 28. Circle or highlight this dollar amount. This amount is the business's net income (NI), and it may be negative or positive. Next you are going to look for the interest expense. On the 2013 Form 1120, interest expense is line 18. Highlight or circle this dollar amount. This amount will represent the business's interest expense (I) paid for existing financing. The interest expense may be zero. You are now going to look for the depreciation amount. Depreciation is line 20 on the 2013 Form 1120. Highlight or circle the amount listed next to depreciation. The depreciation amount may be zero.

You have now found the "NI," the "I," and the "D" of the EBITDA formula. Amortization will be included on the "other deductions" row. If there is a dollar amount listed next to "other deductions" (line 26 of the 2013 Form 1120), you will need to flip through the rest of the tax return to find the schedule where the "other deductions" will be broken out. Other deductions are typically located near the back of the return. If amortization is not listed as an expense, amortization is zero. If it is listed, highlight or circle the dollar amount for amortization (A).

You now have all of the components to compute EBITDA for a business filed on Form 1120. Add "NI" plus "I" plus "D" plus "A," and you will have computed the business's cash flow. If this business is currently leasing its business space from a landlord (paying rent), and the loan request is to purchase or construct a building in which the business will no longer pay rent to a landlord but instead will be making a mortgage payment, you can change EBITDA to EBITDAR. Only in this case are you to circle or highlight this amount listed next to "rent" (line 16 of the 2013 Form 1120) and add the rent (R) amount to EBITDA to calculate cash flow based on EBITDAR. If you will be acquiring this business and you are not currently an owner, you can change EBITDA to EBITDAS. The "S" represents the seller's salary. On the IRS Form 1120, the seller's salary is listed next to "compensation of officers" (line 12 on the 2013 Form 1120). Only in this case are you to circle or highlight this amount listed next to "compensation of officers" and add the sellers salary (S) amount to EBITDA to calculate cash flow based on EBITDAS.

Business Cash Flow—Form 1065(Partnership)

On the Form 1065, you are going to look for the amount listed next to the line item "Ordinary Business Income (Loss)." On the 2013 Form 1065, this is line 22. Circle or highlight this dollar amount. This dollar amount is your net income (NI), and it may be negative or positive. Next you are going to look for the interest expense. On the 2013 Form 1065, this is line 15. Highlight or circle this dollar amount. This amount will represent the business's interest expense (I) paid for existing financing. The interest expense may be zero. You are now going to look for the depreciation amount. Depreciation is 16a on the 2013 Form 1065. Highlight or circle the amount listed next to 16a. The depreciation amount may be zero.

You have now found the "NI," the "I," and the "D" of the EBITDA formula. Amortization will be included in the "other deductions" row. If there is a dollar amount listed next to "other deductions" (line 20 of the 2013 Form 1064), you will need to flip through the rest of the tax return to find the schedule where the "other deductions" will be broken out. Other deductions are typically located near the back of the return. If amortization is not listed as an expense, amortization is zero. If it is listed, highlight or circle the dollar amount.

You now have all of the components to compute EBITDA. Add "NI" plus "I" plus "D" plus "A," and you will have computed the business's cash flow.

If this business is currently leasing its business space from a landlord (paying rent) and the loan request is to purchase or construct a building in which the business will no longer pay rent to a landlord but instead will be making a mortgage payment, you can change EBITDA to EBITDAR. Only in this case, circle or highlight this amount listed next to "rent: other business property" and add the rent (R) amount to EBITDA to calculate cash flow based on EBITDAR. If you will be acquiring this business and you are not currently an owner, you can change EBITDA to EBITDAS. The "S" represents the seller's salary. On the IRS Form 1065, the seller's salary is listed next to "guaranteed payments to partners" (line 10 on the 2013 Form 1065). Only in this case, circle or highlight this amount listed next to "guaranteed payments to partners" and add the seller's salary (S) amount to EBITDA to calculate cash flow based on EBITDAS.

Business Cash Flow—Schedule C of Form 1040, Sole Proprietorship

On the Schedule C, you are going to look for the amount listed next to the line item "Net Profit or (Loss)." On the 2013 Schedule C, this is line 31. Circle or highlight this dollar amount. This dollar amount is your net income (NI), and it may be negative or positive. Next you are going to look for the interest expense. On the 2013 Schedule C, these are lines 16a and 16b. Highlight or circle these dollar amounts. It is most common to only see a dollar amount listed next to 16a, however, add 16a and 16b together. This total will represent the total interest expense (I). The interest expense may be zero. You are now going to look for the depreciation amount. Depreciation is number 13 on the 2013 Schedule C. Highlight or circle this amount. Depreciation may also be zero.

You have now found the "NI," the "I," and the "D" of the EBITDA formula. Amortization will be included in the "other expenses" row. If there is a dollar amount listed next to the "other expenses" row, flip to the next page where all the "other expenses" will be broken out. In some cases, you will see a comment that the "other expenses" are listed on another schedule attached to the tax return. In this case, you will need to find that schedule, which is typically near the back of the tax return. If amortization is not listed as an expense, amortization is zero. If it is listed, highlight or circle the dollar amount.

You now have all of the components to compute EBITDA. Add "NI" plus "I" plus "D" plus "A," and you will have computed the business's cash flow. If this business is currently leasing its business space from a landlord (paying rent) and the loan request is to purchase or construct a building in which the business will no longer pay rent to a landlord, you can change EBITDA to EBITDAR. Only in this case, circle or highlight this amount listed next to "rent: other business property" and add the rent (R) amount to EBITDA to calculate cash flow based on EBITDAR.

Business Cash Flow—Profit and Loss (Income Statement)

On the profit and loss statement, you are going to look at the bottom of the profit and loss section for something that says "Net Income." A profit and loss template is available at www.ApprovedBook.com. Circle or highlight the dollar amount listed next to net income. This dollar amount is the business's net income (NI) and it may be negative or positive. Next you are going to look for the interest expense. On a profit and loss statement, the interest expense will either be located in the primary list of expenses or it may be listed under a shorter list of "other income and expenses," usually near the net income line. Highlight or circle the interest expense dollar amount. This dollar amount will represent the business's interest expense (I) paid for existing financing. The interest expense may be zero. You are now going to look for the depreciation amount. Depreciation may or may not be listed on a profit and loss statement. Highlight or circle the amount listed for depreciation. The depreciation amount may be zero. Last, you are going to look for the amortization (A) expense. This may or may not be listed on a profit and loss. If it is not listed, amortization should be considered to be zero. If amortization is listed on the profit and loss statement, highlight or circle the dollar amount.

You now have all of the components to compute EBITDA for a business represented on a profit and loss statement. Add "NI" plus "I" plus "D" plus "A," and you will have computed the business's cash flow. If this business is currently leasing its business space from a landlord (paying rent) and the loan request is to purchase or construct a building in which the business will no longer pay rent to a landlord but instead will be making a mortgage payment, you can change

EBITDA to EBITDAR. Only in this case, circle or highlight the dollar amount listed next to "rent" or "lease expense" and add the rent (R) amount to EBITDA to calculate cash flow based on EBITDAR. If you will be acquiring this business and you are not currently an owner, you can change EBITDA to EBITDAS. The "S" represents the seller's salary. The seller's salary may be listed as "owner's salary." In many cases, the owner's salary may not be broken out from all wages paid to employees of the company. Getting a copy of the seller's year-to-date (YTD) paystub can justify the amount to be added back for the seller's salary (S). Only if you are purchasing a third party's business are you to circle or highlight the amount listed next to "owner's salary" and add the seller's salary (S) amount to EBITDA to calculate cash flow based on EBITDAS.

Business Cash Flow—Business Acquisition Financing

If your loan request is to purchase someone else's business, the seller and the seller's broker are likely to indicate that you will earn more money than what is represented on the tax return. This may be because some of the expenses listed on the tax return were overstated and/or because personal expenses of the seller such as personal cell phones and personal auto expenses were listed as business expenses. It may also be because the seller did not report all of the income generated by the business on the tax return submitted to the IRS. Both tactics are used by business owners to represent to the taxing authorities that they make less money and thereby to avoid paying taxes. If a seller is willing to attempt to deceive the IRS (with extensive civil and criminal penalties and collection means available to it), it is likely that the seller would have no qualms about deceiving a potential buyer of his business. To protect you, the bank, and the SBA, we have to go by the numbers represented on the tax returns. The returns submitted with the loan request are verified for authenticity by comparing them to the tax return information that was submitted to the IRS. In some cases, additional adjustments to cash flow can be made with supporting evidence. For example, if an employee will be leaving the business following the change in ownership, a W-2 representing that employee's income can justify the amount of salary expense to be added back for employee wages.

Business Debt

The second step to determining business capacity is to review the debt obligations of the business. All debt obligations should be included in the liability section of your business's balance sheet. All debt obligations listed on your balance sheet should be listed on a business debt schedule to keep you organized. If you haven't done so already, prepare a business debt schedule for the business; do so using a template available at www.ApprovedBook.com. All lines of credit and loans paid for by the business should be detailed on a business debt schedule. Exactly how to complete the business debt schedule line by line is detailed in Part Five. If you are requesting financing for the business that you already own, make sure that all debts that your business pays for are detailed on the business debt schedule. If you are purchasing the business and will not be assuming any of the seller's debt, you are going to enter "none" for creditor name and leave the rest of debt information sections blank. The total monthly payments will total at the bottom of the business debt schedule form. Multiply this number times 12 to compute the annual debt payments of the business.

Business Capacity Calculation

Business capacity is the measure of the business's ability to service its debt obligations. Business capacity is calculated by subtracting annual business debt obligations from the business cash flow. If the result is positive, the business is determined to have positive cash flow and if the result is negative, the business is determined to have negative cash flow. If the business has negative cash flow, it will require cash flow to come from other sources such as capital infusions by its owners to avoid insolvency. For example, if you calculated that your business has cash flow of $100,000 and that your business has annual debt service obligations of $60,000, your business would have positive cash flow of $40,000 ($100,000 - $60,000 = $40,000). To simply calculate the cash flow of your business, use the business capacity calculator. A business capacity calculator form is available for download at www.ApprovedBook.com.

Affiliate Business Capacity

In the Personal Capacity section, there is a paragraph on personal ownership in other businesses. Other businesses are considered to be affiliate businesses if you have at least a 20% ownership interest. Affiliate businesses will be considered by the SBA lender in the global analysis discussed in Part Three: Application Capacity. To calculate the business capacity of each of your affiliate businesses, repeat the steps detailed in this Part for all businesses. Up to four businesses can be represented on each business capacity calculator form available at www. ApprovedBook.com.

Business Conditions

Business conditions are the factors that impact the economic stability of a company. Examples of business conditions include recent changes in ownership, changes in management, company involvement in trade organizations and associations, contracts, lease agreements, franchise agreements, customer concentrations, supplier concentrations, lawsuits, theft, increased employee benefit expenses, workers' compensation claims, insurance claims, loan maturities, access to capital, changes in market demand, technology change, market saturation, governmental regulations, disaster recovery, competition, traffic, road construction, demographics around the business location, adequate parking, industry trends, changes in market positioning, seasonality, weather, product delays, sales cycles, employee deaths, employee resignations, employee additions, employee absences, judgments, liens, sales trends, income statement ratios, balance sheet ratios, external sources of revenue and expense, Internet and media reviews, and many more.

To determine business conditions, we are going to discuss how lenders will evaluate your industry, your business's financial statements, your company history, and your business plan. The first step to determine the conditions of a business is to evaluate the financials of the company. The second step is to obtain company and industry information from the Internet. The third and most important step is where the lender will attempt to predict the future outlook for your industry and the subject business.

Financial Condition Analysis

When a lender analyzes your business, the last three years of tax returns and the current interim financial statements (representing the time between the most recently filed tax return and the present) will be analyzed. Each line item will be compared year to year. The lender will look for continued sales growth, stable or declining costs of goods sold, stable or declining operating expenses, and stable or increasing profit. It should be noted that many businesses considered for financing do not reflect perfect financial trends. In addition, lenders will generate financial ratios from the business financials to highlight irregularities in the income statements, balance sheets, and other financial documents. Be prepared to speak about why dollar amounts differ from one year to another. Expect questions about why sales are up or down, why the company experienced a loss, or why revenue was unusually high or low one year. Also have a good understanding of the company's assets, such as machinery and equipment, and its liabilities, such as loan balances and terms. The lender wants to justify that any abnormalities in your financial history are unlikely to occur in the future to the detriment of your business.

Industry Analysis

In addition to reading information about the business and industry that you, the applicant, provide, the lender will do its own research on the company and industry. Industry and company research will include ordering industry reports from companies such as IBISWorld and Hoover's. City, county, state, and federal records will be ordered to determine outstanding taxes, lawsuits, judgments, and liens filed against a company. The company will also be searched on the Internet to discover competitors, customer reviews, and additional information regarding factors influencing and affecting the business.

The Grey Area

Every lender may perceive your business, industry, and future outlook differently. Varied perceptions are due to the individual lender's experience with your industry, statistical models, media, and a million other sources that can fog the reality of your business. Conditions are the grey area where a loan can be approved or declined based on a lender's level of understanding of (and comfort with) your business, industry, and the factors influencing it. Lenders are risk adverse and if they have a negative perception about the future outlook of your company based on business conditions, loan approval can be a challenge. Reading financial statements for lenders is easy. Reading a credit report to determine if a person pays their bills is easy. Expecting a lender to have a thorough understanding of an industry outside of banking or the factors that impact your business's economic stability is not realistic. To substantially reduce the lender's anxiety about lending to your business and industry that may not be well understood, industry and company information that would be found in a business plan should be provided. Completing the business plan questionnaire detailed in Part Four will answer the majority of the lender's questions about your business and industry. Most of the questions in the questionnaire are questions that you will be asked by the lender anyway, so you will save time by completing the questionnaire. The business plan questionnaire can be downloaded from www.ApprovedBook.com.

The SBA mitigation

To score well for business conditions when applying for a loan, you want the business to be perceived as stable, steadily growing, well managed, diversified among suppliers and customers, free of lawsuits, properly insured, in a growing industry, having low employee turnover, and predictable. Considering that few businesses are immune to a constantly changing economy and all of the other factors impacting a business, business conditions are one of the most common reasons why lenders rely on the SBA program when making business loans. The SBA guaranty provided to lenders enables them to mitigate most of the uncertainty for future business performance. Regardless of the conditions impacting your business, the SBA guaranty substantially reduces lender's loan risk.

Business Capital

Business capital represents the business's sources of working capital. From the lender's perspective, liquid assets are the best sources of business working capital as they can quickly be used for needs such as covering payroll. Liquid assets include cash, marketable securities such as stocks and bonds, and accounts receivable. Business capital can be used for several purposes in addition to operating expenses, such as investing in marketing, new employees, and new equipment, or as reserves to cover fluctuations in income and expenses. Business capital can also be used by the owners to invest in other companies. It is a common source of equity contributed toward a project to be financed with an SBA loan. Most SBA lenders require at least a 10% equity injection toward a financed project. In addition to initial capital injections, business capital will also be evaluated by the SBA lender as a source of ongoing capital for the business. Access to working capital is critical for the success of any business.

To evaluate business capital, we are going to discuss the business's balance sheet. All businesses involved in a business loan application will be evaluated for business capital based on their respective balance sheet. Lenders consider the balance sheet to be the primary source of information to evaluate business capital. While the balance sheet is a very important document from the lender's perspective, it's completely misunderstood by most entrepreneurs. Don't worry; if you cannot answer a question about your balance sheet, your accountant will understand it and it is common to have your accountant and lender speak directly to keep the process rolling. In addition, many lenders can help you reconstruct a more accurate balance sheet based on a bank statement and other information collected in the application process.

Balance Sheet

Sources of capital listed on the business's balance sheet include cash, checking accounts, savings accounts, CDs, money market accounts, marketable securities, retirements accounts, accounts receivable, notes receivable, inventory, equipment, equity in real estate, business credit cards, and business lines of credit. Business assets such as real estate, trucks, and equipment can be sold and converted to cash to generate capital for a business. Many businesses raise capital by offering special promotions/prices to generate a surge of sales when cash is tight. As an alternative and often in conjunction with applying for business credit (business loans), many entrepreneurs seek to raise capital by selling equity interests in a company. Selling equity in a company to raise capital can be a relatively simple solution, but there are negatives and positives. Investments by minority shareholders can raise substantial capital; however, management control may suffer and personal guaranties will be required from any investors with at least a 20% equity interest in the business.

Equity Injection
Details about any money previously invested by a business toward a new project to be financed should be communicated to the lender. As mentioned previously, it's common for entrepreneurs to get excited about a new project and start buying "stuff" such as equipment before a loan application has been approved. At the time of application, your SBA lender should tell you to freeze (to the extent possible) your project spending until underwriting has been completed. This enables the lender to catch up and document everything properly and eliminate a moving application. Moving applications are applications that continually change, resulting in your loan officer and the underwriting department having a difficult time determining the total project cost as well as what to allocate for the new loan and for equity injection. The SBA lender wants to credit the business and owners for every dollar invested toward a project. Tens of thousands of dollars can be missed during the application process due to failures of communication and documentation failure between applicant and lender about previously invested capital. This includes hard costs such as land or equipment and soft costs such as architect fees and other professional fees.

Capital Analysis
When analyzing a business's capital position, a commercial lender will run several calculations. These calculations include working capital ratio, quick ratio, current ratio, and leverage ratio. To calculate a company's working capital based on the balance sheet, current liabilities are subtracted from current assets. The quick ratio measures a company's ability to pay its current liabilities solely based on the total cash and accounts receivable on the balance sheet. Similar to the working capital calculation, the current ratio compares the current assets to the current liabilities of the company but as a percentage. The debt to equity ratio

compares the total amount of liabilities to the amount of equity in a business. As assets increase and liabilities are decreased, equity increases. Many SBA loans are considered to be highly leveraged because of lack of tangible collateral. As discussed in Part One, the SBA is a common mitigation source for businesses having ratios outside of a lender's comfort level.

Business Collateral

Business collateral is what lenders use to secure a loan as a secondary source of repayment if the business were to fail. Lenders love collateral because they are risk adverse. Due to lack of collateral, many business owners would not be able to obtain financing if it wasn't for the assistance of the SBA. Regardless of the amount of collateral available to secure a loan, the collateral will always be the lender's second source of repayment if a business were to fail even if the loan amount is much greater than the collateral value. To determine your business collateral, your balance sheet, business debt schedule, and schedule of collateral will be reviewed. UCC and lien searches will also be performed by the lender and third-party companies to determine all outstanding liens against your collateral.

Balance Sheet

As discussed in the business capital section, the balance sheet is one of the most important documents that lenders evaluate when determining if they will loan your business money. The balance sheet gives the lender a snapshot of all of your business's assets, its liabilities, and equity as of a single date. For example, let's say you just purchased a building and some manufacturing equipment to start a company to produce pencils. You purchased the building for $500,000. You invested $100,000 of your money toward the purchase of the building and obtained a loan for $400,000. You purchased the manufacturing equipment for $200,000. You were able to obtain financing for 50% of the equipment purchase price so you obtained a loan for $100,000 and invested another $100,000 of your own money. So how would this look on your balance sheet? You would have $700,000 of assets (building worth $500,000 plus equipment worth $200,000). You would have $500,000 of liabilities or debt (building loan of $400,000 and equipment loan of $100,000). You would have equity of $200,000, which is the total amount of money that you invested toward the building and equipment. Obviously your balance sheet is likely to have additional line items than are in this example, however, this is a basic balance sheet. From the lender's perspective, it is easy to determine that you have $700,000 of assets, $500,000 in liabilities, and $200,000 of equity. Without any appraisals, environmental studies, closing costs, or anything else, the lender can evaluate if it is comfortable making additional loans to you based on the remaining $200,000 in equity in the business. The lender can also evaluate if it wants to offer you better terms than what you currently have on the equipment or real estate loan.

After comparing this basic balance sheet to your business's balance sheet, you may become completely confused again due to unfamiliar items such as amortization, depreciation, and several other line items listed in the assets, liabilities, and equity sections of the balance sheet.

Like most entrepreneurs, allocating assets, liabilities, and equity on your internal company- prepared balance sheet may not be your expertise or passion, so errors are common. Many balance sheets fail to list assets that can be used by lenders as collateral. Thank goodness there are accountants to correct your books for tax time. Considering that many entrepreneurs have difficulty preparing a balance sheet correctly, the SBA requires that two other documents, which are much simpler to complete than a balance sheet, be submitted as part of the application process. These include the business debt schedule and the schedule of collateral. Both of these forms are available for download from www. ApprovedBook.com.

Business Debt Schedule

A business debt schedule is to be completed for the applicant business as well as for all other businesses in which you have a 20% or greater ownership interest. For each business, you will list all of the loans for which the business is liable. This includes all of the loans and lines of credit on which you signed a loan agreement and on which the business makes regular payments. Some business debt schedules also ask you to enter all of your long-term lease agreements. Short-term liabilities such as accounts payable, payroll, and general expenses are not to be included on the business debt schedule. Once completed, the business debt schedule will provide you and your lender with a snapshot of all of your business loans, including valuable information such as monthly payment, interest rate, loan balance, and collateral. For detailed instructions for how to complete the business debt schedule, see Part Five.

Schedule of Collateral

After completing the business debt schedule, the next step is to complete a schedule of collateral. While the balance sheet gives the lender a good idea of the total value of a company's assets, it is usually difficult for the lender to determine what physical and intangible assets are actually represented on the balance sheet. To address this issue and also to take into consideration assets that were forgotten to be recorded on the balance sheet, the SBA requires a schedule of collateral to be submitted. The SBA requires that the schedule of collateral include all company assets with a value of at least $5,000. I recommend listing all of your assets with a value of $1,000 or greater. The list should include all of your company's real estate, company cars, your machinery and equipment, furniture and fixtures. It will also indicate your estimate of current value, serial numbers, whether the asset is pledged as collateral, and other information useful to determine collateral that may enable you to get additional funding. If you own an intangible asset such as a liquor license or patent, that asset should also be listed. Keep in mind that while a lender never wants to sell your collateral to try to get its money back, it makes them feel much better about making you a loan if there is some sort of secondary repayment.

CHAPTER 8

THE SBA APPLICATION CREDIT PROFILE

The application credit profile is a hierarchical look at an SBA application. It starts at the top with the application request and then drills down to the business and the individuals that support it. From a character perspective, *application character* compares the management needs of the business to the character profiles of the individual applicants. From the capacity perspective, *application capacity* compares the cash flow requirements of the requested loan amount to the cash flow generated by the business less the individual income requirements of the applicant business owners. *Application capital* compares the total financing project cost and equity injection requirements to the sources of capital available. For conditions, *application conditions* is an evaluation of the factors influencing the individual applicants and business and how they will impact the success of the SBA loan application. *Application collateral* is an evaluation of the SBA loan request and all available business and personal collateral that will be required to be pledged to meet SBA collateral requirements.

In this section, the strengths and weaknesses of the various facets of the application are considered to determine a feasible structure to reach the goals of the application profile. Traditional commercial loan agreements are full of lender favorable conditions enabling lenders to get out of the loans that they have made to you. To your favor, SBA loans are granted to you until they are paid in full, similar to most residential loans. That being said, the SBA lender only gets one chance (at time of application) to decide if it wants to get in bed with you for the entire term of the loan. Again, banks are risk adverse and businesses change over the years, so to commit to a borrower for up to 25 years in many cases can be difficult for most lenders to swallow. The SBA has made this much easier for lenders in that lenders typically have at least a 50% guaranty from the government. If you default on your SBA loan, the lender is only at risk for the unguarantied percentage of the loan loss.

In this Chapter, you will learn how the SBA and SBA lender will evaluate your loan request and the supporting documents discussed in Chapter 6 and Chapter 7. In addition to previously discussed documents, the following documents will be discussed in this Chapter, including:

- Business Loan Application Summary template (download template)
- Sources and Uses of Funds template (download template)
- Business Information and History template (download template)
- Business Capacity Calculator (download template)
- Application Capacity Calculator (download template)
- Business Plan (download Business Plan Questionnaire template)
- Financial Projections template (download template)
- Contracts and agreements subject to the application

All template forms can be downloaded from www.ApprovedBook.com.

Application Character

Application character is the synergy between personal character and business character. Application character is determined by evaluating the character of all of the individual applicants and the character requirements of the applicant business. Many loan applications are declined solely based on the misalignment between these two critical components. To evaluate application character, SBA lenders will compare the management requirements of the business with the expertise and credit of the applicant principals.

As the SBA lender learns about the business and the applicants, several questions will be asked. Will the SBA and SBA lender be confident that the parties involved in this application will do whatever it takes to repay the loan? Do the parties involved have the experience to run the business successfully? For a change of ownership, will the new business owners do at least as well as the seller?

Résumé and Transferrable Experience

Effective management is critical for business success. After the lender gets a high-level understanding of the business and the credit reports of the individual applicants, the lender will turn to the résumés. On the résumé available to be downloaded from www.ApprovedBook.com, the second page asks pointed questions where you can detail your transferable experience related to the applicant business. It is critical to identify how the individual loan applicants meet the management requirements of the applicant business. You will be asked by the SBA lender to identify which principals of the application (will) perform which of the responsibilities of the applicant business. The experience detailed in each of the principal's résumés must justify the position (to be) held at the applicant business.

Credit Reports

After receiving an application request, lenders will order credit reports on the individuals identified to have at least a 20% interest in the applicant company. Applicants with credit scores in the high 700s to 850 range are great to see, but it's common to see scores in the mid 700s or lower. The high scores require little explanation while the scores less than 700 require increasingly more scrutiny. I personally go over credit reports line by line with my customers because I want to make sure my applicants and I are on the same page. Even the applicants in the 800s have items to be addressed on the credit report, such as loan balances. Due to timing and other factors influencing the credit report, credit report information may be inconsistent with what an applicant's report should reflect. During my conversation with borrowers, I will recommend paying off or reducing balances on certain accounts to improve personal cash flow and their credit score. Errors on the credit report should be clarified by statements and documents that are easily obtained from creditors.

Character Issues

When matching up the individual applicants with the business loan request, lenders do their best to identify the members who are good and those who are not as good. A low credit score, limited personal liquidity, arrest history, financial problems, gambling problems, lawsuits, and more will be identified during the application process. Issues identified late in the process are both frustrating and uncomfortable for all parties, as the success of an application request can be in jeopardy due to character issues.

The individual applicants listed on a business loan application can be compared to the students in a grade school class. The students who are excelling are often held back by students who are struggling to keep up. Similarly, the success of a loan application can be broken based on its weakest link. When it comes to loans, weak links can be deal killers. Four 20% owners of a business can be stellar, but if the remaining 20% owner is weak, bounces checks, gets in trouble with the law, doesn't care to pay bills, etc., delays in processing should be expected. Applications submitted with owners who have character issues need to expect delays, additional documentation, and questions that ultimately may lead to loan decline.

Prior to finalizing partnership agreements, get everything on the table. Identify the strengths and weaknesses of everyone involved. Before determining ownership, identify potential issues for all of the 20% or greater owners and plan accordingly for potential delays. The SBA is extremely flexible with its qualification requirements, and thousands of people with questionable backgrounds get SBA loans; however, additional steps may need to be taken to get to the closing table, including applying to several lenders. If issues are identified, consider using a loan broker to help you identify lenders that are more flexible with character issues.

New Entities

It is common for new entities to be formed for the purpose of SBA financing. This is common when there is a change in ownership, a business is expanding through purchase of assets such as real estate, or a new business is planned to be established. As previously mentioned, character is the most important factor for a small business. A bad egg can spoil the whole carton. If it is determined that an individual's "Personal Character" (as discussed in Chapter 6) may negatively impact a loan application, careful consideration should be given to the amount of ownership interest to be held by that individual.

Application Capacity

Application capacity is the final step in determining capacity. Application capacity includes the combined analysis of the personal capacity of each of the SBA loan application guarantors, the business capacity of the applicant business, and the business capacity of all of the affiliate businesses owned by SBA loan application guarantors. The application capacity analysis will provide you with the gross cash flow amount that the SBA lender will use to determine the amount of SBA financing that can be offered.

Step 1: Gross Personal Capacity

The first step to determine application capacity is to compile the personal capacity of all of the guarantors of the SBA loan request. As discussed in Part Two, the SBA will require all 20% owners to guaranty SBA loan requests. Additional guarantors with less than 20% ownership may be required depending on circumstances discussed in Part Two. All guarantors (jointly with spouses) are to prepare personal income and expense templates as discussed in Chapter 6 (Personal Capacity). The cash flow surplus (deficit) dollar amount specified in the pro forma column on the personal income and expense worksheet for each of the guarantors is to be added together. The total represents the owner salary that must be supported by the applicant business. This calculation can be prepared on the Application Capacity Calculator available at www.ApprovedBook.com. Keep in mind that a deficit is far more common that a surplus as it is expected that the owners of the applicant business will need to draw a salary from that business.

The total amount will be represented as gross personal capacity. The deficit can be several hundred thousand dollars depending on the number of owners relying on the business to support their lifestyle.

Step 2: Gross Business Capacity

The second step to determine application capacity is to compile the business capacity (cash flow) of all of the businesses and affiliate businesses discussed in Chapter 7 (Business Capacity). Any business debt (listed on the business debt schedule) to be refinanced as part of the SBA loan request should not be included on the annual debt service (DS) line of the *business capacity calculator*. For businesses with debt to be refinanced, the pro forma column should be used to recalculate business cash flow. To recalculate business cash flow in the pro forma column, copy all of the EBITDARS numbers to the pro forma column so that the gross cash flow (GCF) total is the same. For the annual debt service, only include the debts listed on the business debt schedule that will *not* be refinanced as part of the loan request. Subtract the pro forma annual debt service (DS) from the pro forma gross cash flow (GCF) to determine the new cash flow (CF) for the business as if the debt to be refinanced does not exist. For each of the businesses, list the cash flow (or pro forma cash flow for businesses with debt to be refinanced) and business name on the application capacity calculator in the business capacity section. All of this can be performed using the *application capacity calculator* available at www.ApprovedBook. com. The gross business cash flow listed on the *application capacity calculator* represents the total cash flow available to service the SBA loan request (without consideration of personal capacity).

Step 3: Application Capacity

The third step to determine application capacity is to add the gross personal capacity (typically a negative number) and the gross business capacity together. The resulting application capacity represents the total amount of cash flow available to service the new SBA loan. The application capacity dollar amount calculated is in its basic format of gross cash flow. It is typical that lenders require more gross cash flow than the annual dollar amount for new debt payments. The

SBA requires that all loans in excess of $350,000 have gross cash flow that is at least 115% of the new annual loan payments. The bottom of the application capacity calculator provides several "debt-to-income" ratios ranging from 100% debt-to-income to 150% debt-to-income.

SBA Loan Amount and Terms

Loan amount, terms, and conditions are detailed in Part Two. As a rule of thumb, real estate is typically financed over 25 years and at 90% LTV. Business acquisition loans are typically financed over 10 years and at 75% of the business valuation. Loans for any purpose other than real estate or business acquisition are typically financed over 10 years and up to 100% LTV. Loans that are for multiple purposes, including real estate, closing costs, and another purpose, are typically financed over a blended term between 10 and 25 years. Most banks price their loans based on a spread over the Wall Street Journal (WSJ) prime rate, and it is typically WSJ-Prime + 2.75%. As of the writing of this book, WSJ-Prime was 3.25%, resulting in a loan rate of 6.0%. You can determine the monthly payment of your requested loan amount by using a financial calculator or by visiting www.ApprovedBook.com.

Insufficient Application Capacity

In situations where the gross cash flow (income) represented by the application capacity amount is inadequate to support the annual debt payments of the requested SBA loan, a couple of options may be available. For business acquisitions, if the loan amount is not supported by historical cash flow, the lender is likely to offer a lower loan amount. A reduced loan amount typically will require additional equity injection (capital) that is detailed in the application capital section of this Chapter. In situations where the cash flow is insufficient to support a loan request for a change of ownership, it is unlikely that the business valuation will support the purchase price. In that situation, the buyer may wish to attempt to renegotiate the contract price.

For applicant businesses requesting SBA financing by their existing owners, a second option supported by financial projections is common. As discussed in Part One and Part Two, an SBA loan can be approved based on a historical or *projected* cash flow basis. To determine the amount of additional gross cash flow that the business must generate to support the larger SBA loan request, you can make adjustments on the application capacity calculator. The easiest way to do this is to list the applicant business name on another line in the business capacity section with "expansion" listed next to it. You will then add a new capacity dollar figure to the right in the business capacity column. Increase the new business capacity number until the requested loan amount payment is between the 1.35:1 and 1.50:1 gross cash flow to debt ratio for monthly payment. If you feel confident that your business can increase its bottom line by the new "expansion" dollar amount, do the exercises in Part Four that walk you through how to prepare a business plan, financial projections, and projection assumptions.

Application Conditions

Application conditions are the factors in your personal life and business life that make a lender excited or nervous about the long-term success of your business. What is going on in your life that will impact the business negatively? Are you in a lawsuit that will affect your ability to manage the business effectively? Will the change in ownership cause key employee turnover? Will the move to the new location benefit or damage the reputation of the company? Will traffic increase or decrease? How will new technology impact your business? Why is the seller getting out of the business?

"Conditions" are often poorly evaluated due to lack of industry knowledge by a lender and lack of information provided by an applicant. Business plans, projections, contract terms, and program eligibility will be evaluated to determine the application conditions.

Business Overview

The first step to determine application conditions is for the lender to get a general understanding of the business and the industry with which it transacts business. Several of the eligibility requirements of SBA lending will be evaluated at this stage, such as whether the business is in operation (or about to be), it's for profit, it's located in the United States, and it's a business type not excluded as an ineligible business. Once the industry is identified, additional red flags may come up if the industry is known to be of high risk, such as the restaurant industry.

Application Request

The second step is to determine the goal of the loan request and the actual objectives of the parties involved. Many loan applications are submitted without a clear request detailing the proposed use of the loan proceeds. Once the goal is determined, several options internal and external to the SBA loan programs may be considered.

Conditions Evaluation

The third step is digging into the story of the transaction. What are the factors influencing the transaction? Why is the seller selling? What are the time constraints? Do the applicants have character issues such as an arrest history or bad credit? Are there any tricky conditions in the contract? Is the landlord willing to extend the term of the lease to match the term of the loan? Will the seller extend the purchase contract closing date to satisfy the appraisal time requirements? Is the business a franchise? How will the appraisal and environmental reports impact the project? Are their existing liens on the business assets or real estate proposed to be taken as collateral? Can the major stockholder get life insurance? Is the property in a flood zone? Does the business plan make sense? Are the financial projections reasonable and supported by assumptions? Are the applicants responsive with providing information? Is a signing authority on vacation? Are there other loans on an underwriter's desk that are taking priority over your loan request?

There can be a hundred different conditions that impact the success of an application. Good lenders are good at keeping the ball moving forward despite the bumps along the way. Do your very best to be an open book, with full disclosure throughout the loan approval process. Your loan officer should hold your hand throughout it to deliver you loan approval in the most efficient manner possible.

Application Capital

Application capital is an evaluation of the personal capital and business capital to meet the capital requirements of the requested financing. For example, if the loan request is for a start-up business requiring total project financing of $2 million, the lender may require a capital contribution of at least 20% to 30%. The lender will total the amount of available capital listed on the applicant's personal financial statements to see if the equity requirement is available. For real estate purchases, most lenders require an equity injection of at least 10%. In this case, the lender will look at the personal financial statements and business balance sheets to determine if a 10% injection is feasible. In all cases, the lender will total the liquid sources listed on the owner's personal financial statements, the business's balance sheet, and the affiliated business's balance sheets to determine if the required equity injection is available.

If the required equity injection is not available based on the various business balance sheets and personal financial statements, additional sources of capital may be an option. As discussed in the personal capital section, personal assets can be sold to generate capital. A second mortgage or line of credit on personal real estate can also be borrowed against to generate capital. Another common source of capital for an SBA loan comes in the form of gifts. Families commonly give gifts of money for the purpose of down payment for SBA loans. Gifts are great because they are not loans (debt), and they never need to be repaid. A fourth option to raise capital is to sell small equity interests in the applicant business.

At the onset of any loan request, lenders will always look at the balance sheet and personal financial statements to determine if adequate capital is available for the requested loan. If the required equity injection is not represented, it is common for lenders to put your application on the bottom of the pile. Make sure that the source of your equity injection is clearly indicated. Also, clearly indicate all money previously invested with documentation. Getting all of the money in a bank account early in the process will also reduce lots of paperwork and questions. The SBA requires that the sources of equity injection be identified and verified. This means that bank statements for the two months prior to the month in which the loan is funded must show that the down payment funds have been available.

Application Collateral

Application collateral represents all of the personal and business collateral available to secure the SBA loan. The goal of application collateral is to secure the SBA loan by all eligible collateral up to the point that the SBA would consider the loan to be fully secured (if possible). Keep in mind that many loans considered to be fully secured by SBA rules are undersecured by conventional standards. Also note that many SBA loans and especially SBA loans that financed changes of ownership are highly undersecured due to lack of available collateral.

After calculating the total project cost of a financial transaction represented in the application, a lender will determine the amount of collateral available to secure the loan in case the business were to fail. As mentioned, an SBA loan may not be declined solely because of inadequate collateral if the other factors of the application support the request. That being said, lenders love collateral and the SBA permits lenders to collateralize SBA loans with personal and business assets.

To be sure that the SBA lender has full understanding of the collateral available to help secure the SBA loan, make sure to fully complete the personal financial statement, personal financial statement addendum (as necessary), schedule of collateral, and business debt schedules. All of these templates are available at www.ApprovedBook.com. Detailed information about how to complete the personal financial statement and business debt schedule is included in Part Five. Information about how to complete all forms discussed in this book is available at www.ApprovedBook.com.

If the value of a piece of collateral listed on the schedule of collateral far exceeds the net book value of the collateral as listed on the balance sheet, the lender may require you to have the collateral appraised. It is common for equipment to be depreciated at a faster rate than the actual useful life of the equipment. In these cases it may make sense to incur the expense of obtaining the appraisal especially if it will enable you to get a larger loan amount. While the SBA does not require equipment to be appraised, they do allow lenders to allocate a much higher value to appraised assets that may encourage them to offer a larger loan amount.

CHAPTER 9

THE SBA LENDER CREDIT PROFILE

In Chapter 6, you learned all about how you and your partners will be evaluated under the personal profile. In Chapter 7, you learned how the applicant business will be evaluated in the business credit profile. In the SBA application profile chapter (Chapter 8), you learned how the application request will be evaluated as it relates to the combination of the personal and business credit profiles. There is a fourth credit profile yet to be described. This profile is called the SBA lender credit profile. The SBA lender credit profile is unique to each SBA lender. As mentioned in other areas of the book, no lender is the same. The SBA lender credit profile is how each SBA lender bridges its own unique credit policy to SBA's credit policy (the SBA's standard operating policy) as detailed in Part Two.

The SBA lender credit policy tends to be a moving target as lenders become hot, cold, open, and closed. No SBA lender is ever the same, and each SBA lender's policy changes frequently and sometimes drastically. This makes it very difficult to detail in a book because requirements are updated and information often becomes obsolete and outdated. That being said, I keep an active database of SBA lenders across the country. To find an SBA lender in your area, visit www. ApprovedBook.com.

SBA lenders continually change and evolve for several reasons. Regulation has dramatically increased over the last several years, keeping lenders on their toes as they never know when the next audit will happen. Lenders each have unique credit policies that detail what types of loan transactions they are willing to make and on what terms and conditions they will be offered. Some lenders like to be fully secured by collateral; others are driven by cash flow. Some lenders are sticklers for credit score; others understand life circumstances. Some SBA lenders like start-up businesses and expansions, while others like only professional practices.

Lender portfolio concentrations continually change as a lender may get an influx of applications in one type of industry and then need to shut the door on that industry and market for something else. Portfolio diversification keeps the regulators away. There are several industries, such as restaurants and hotels, which some lenders completely avoid while other lenders seek them out. When a lender has a bad experience with a particular industry, such as when it is dealing with defaults by several businesses in that industry, lending to such businesses is usually halted until the lender's comfort level is restored.

In the SBA loan business, SBA experts frequently move from one SBA lender to another, so finding an SBA lender with knowledgeable, experienced, and dedicated personnel qualified to meet your needs can be a challenge. If you are unsure of which SBA lender is the best fit for your particular request, visit www.ApprovedBook.com.

PART FOUR
THE BUSINESS PLAN QUESTIONNAIRE

I have met very few entrepreneurs who were excited about writing a business plan. The thought of writing a business plan actually causes many entrepreneurs to experience anxiety and/or nausea. You're a visionary and excited to get going with your new business or growth opportunity. For these reasons, I have designed this business plan Part (and downloadable forms) to be straightforward, easy to complete, and enormously helpful for obtaining financing for your business. Whether you are looking to obtain a business loan to fund your project, raise equity to fund it, or a combination of the two, Part Four addresses the key business plan items that lenders and investors require to decide whether to fund your request.

The business plan questionnaire was designed to provide the lender with the specific information about your company most relevant to approving your business loan application. The questionnaire starts with general information about the company and industry and then drills down into the specifics of why your business will (or continues to) experience growth and profitability. Fewer questions will be asked in some sections and more in others to address what SBA lenders care most about. For new businesses, the goal of the business plan is to convince lenders (and investors) that your business will be profitable relatively quickly and will be successful for the long term. For existing businesses with a growth opportunity, the business plan is intended to convince lenders (and investors) that your business will be able to increase profitability and support all debt obligations.

To obtain financing for a new business (or a business that lacks historical tax returns that support the financing request), lenders require you to provide a business plan. A business plan is highly recommended for start-up and growing businesses for two purposes. The first is to provide you (and potential lenders/ investors) with a written plan for how you are going to operate your business consistently. The second reason is to enable potential lenders and investors to evaluate if your business idea will have the capacity to generate an adequate profit to support your requested loan or investment.

A successful business transitions through three phases summarized by three types of business plans. These business plans are a financing plan, an operating plan, and an exit plan. The financing plan is what is presented to a lender (or investor) to obtain financing. The operating plan is what you are going to use on a daily basis to manage your business. The exit plan is what your operating plan will eventually become once systems and processes are fine-tuned, enabling you to remove yourself from the operation. Once the exit plan has been completed, business sale and franchising is more easily pursued. Considering that you desire financing, the business plan questionnaire focuses on the most basic plan: the financing plan.

The business plan questionnaire has 10 sections plus appendices for reference information such as product brochures. The sections are: company summary, industry analysis, target market analysis, competition, products and services, sales and marketing, management and organization, operations plan, financial plan, and executive summary. Each section includes five to 15 questions that will be used by the lender for business analysis and discussion. Complete the questionnaire from front to back as the questions within each section build on information collected in preceding sections. If a question is not applicable, write "N/A." If you are not sure how to answer a question, skip it and come back. Try to answer all applicable questions using bullets to avoid lengthy paragraphs. Once you have gone through the plan from front to back the first time, flip back and forth between the sections to provide additional information to questions that were either skipped or could be more thoroughly answered.

As mentioned, the business plan questionnaire has 10 sections. The company summary provides an overview of the company including a product and service overview, location, and ownership. The industry analysis gives you the opportunity to describe the industry, the trends, the barriers to competitors, and trade association information. The target market analysis defines your target market. It describes who your customers are. In the competition section and accompanying competition analysis template, you will evaluate your competition on a macro and micro level. Strengths and weaknesses discovered here will help you define your "go-to market" strategy. In the products and services section, you will provide a summary for the niche of products and services that you sell. The summary will include information on technology, quality, competitive advantages, suppliers and vendors, and production timeline. Brochures on company products and services should be included in the appendices section at the end of the business plan questionnaire. The sales and marketing section is all about conversion of your product and services into sales. This includes customer makeup, pricing, sales channels, and general marketing.

The management and organizational plan provides an overview of the labor chart from top to bottom. Having a good understanding of roles and responsibilities as well as how to obtain and retain good employees will be discussed. The operations plan is a high-level summary of how the company's engine operates. Once funding has been obtained, it is recommended that this section of the plan be fully developed. The financial plan is the most important section of the questionnaire. The questions address what will be asked by lenders as they relate to the cash flow of the business. Any reports related to the future financial profitability (e.g., feasibility study and/or financial projections) should be included in the appendices section at the end of the questionnaire. The executive summary is a summary of everything previously discussed in the other sections. The executive summary and financial projections discussed in Part Five are typically the starting point of discussion between you and your lender. The appendices (at the back of the questionnaire) are for reference information to support your answers provided in the questionnaire.

CHAPTER 10

THE BUSINESS PLAN QUESTIONNAIRE

Company Summary

1. What types of products and services does the company sell?
2. What are all of the trade names by which the company transacts business? (Websites, company names, corporation names, brand names)
3. What is the physical address of the main business office? How many other locations are there?
4. Does the business lease or own its location? What is the amount, in square feet of the space, occupied by the business?
5. When was the company formed? By whom?
6. Who are the existing owners of the company (name, title, ownership)?
7. Have there been any recent changes in ownership? When? (Detail the circumstances)
8. How many full- and part-time employees work for the company?
9. What copyrights, trademarks, or patents are owned by the company?

10. Under what contracts, franchise agreements, or license agreements does the company operate?

11. What have been the sources of funding for the business to date? (Source and amount)

12. What assets are owned by the company? (See schedule of collateral template)

Industry Analysis

1. What is the company's NAICS code?

   NAICS stands for North American Industry Classification System. This is a six-digit "business activity code number" that identifies your industry. This number is listed on your business tax return. If you do not have a code or to verify the accuracy of the code number listed on your business tax return, go to www.naicscodelookup.com. Choose the best NAICS code based on your products, services, and target market.

2. What trends in the industry have created opportunities for your company? (Technology, economy, etc.)

3. What is the growth rate of your industry?

   To find this, Google your industry with "growth rate" after your industry-related search terms. Also check out free websites such as www.sbdcnet.org. Information will also be posted on industry-related websites. Print out relevant articles about the industry.

4. What are the barriers to entry for the industry? (Technology, large capital requirements, personnel expertise, licensing, regulation, patents, start-up costs, etc.)

5. What trade organizations and associations target your industry? (Include trade magazines and trade websites)

   To find trade organizations, associations, trade magazines, and trade websites, search keywords (e.g., "childcare" for daycare services). For each keyword searched, click through each of the sites listed for the first five to 10 pages of results (including advertisements). List the organizations, associations, magazines, and websites that are most relevant to your industry. Note that the websites that show up in pages one through 10 of Google are the sites most highly visited (by your customers). The better you stay up to date with the information presented by these websites, the more aligned you and your business plan will be with your target market. In addition, make note of all of the competitors and potential competitors that are serving your trade area. You will use this competition information to complete the competition section of your business plan.

6. What is the industry outlook for your business? What do your trade organizations predict?

   Search the Internet for articles relevant to your industry. Your local librarian can be extremely helpful for this type of research. Barnes & Noble is likely to have your industry magazines.

7. What is your company's reputation in the industry?

Target Market Analysis

1. Who is your target market? What type of person or business wants your products/services?

2. What customer problem (pain) does your business solve?

3. Describe your target consumer customer. (Age, income, gender, location, occupation, marital status, family size, education level, hobbies, children, ethnic origin, religion, race, job title, home ownership, interests, etc.)

4. Describe your target business customers. (Industries, years in business, number of employees, revenues, etc.)

5. What geographic area does your business serve? (Block radius, zip code, city, county, state, etc.)

6. Describe the geographic area. (Neighborhood, population, demographics, traffic, and seasonality)

   You can find demographic information by searching the zip code followed by "demographics" in Google.

7. Describe your business location. (Neighboring businesses, traffic, access, parking, visibility)

8. What is the population size of your target market in the geographic area that you serve?

   Once you have identified your geographic market and your customer profile, you can use population statistics to estimate your target market population.

9. Is the concentration of your target market increasing or decreasing (neighborhood demographics change)? What is the growth rate?

Competition

1. What are the types of businesses that compete with you? What are the advantages and disadvantages of these types of competing businesses? (See competition analysis template)

   Competition types may include door-to-door salespeople, web-based businesses, retail operators, small companies, and large conglomerates. List all of the possible types of businesses that could solve the market need. Think of companies with similar products and services to you as well as companies that offer very different products and services that provide a similar solution for the customer. The advantages and disadvantages could be price, product features, quality, selection, customer service, warranties, reliability, expertise, reputation, convenience, marketing, brand, contracts, efficiencies, capital, technology, bureaucracy, or others. Use the competitive analysis template available at www.ApprovedBook.com to complete this section.

2. What are the top 10 companies that you consider to be direct competition? List the company name, type of competitor (above), their market share percentage, location and website. (See competition analysis template)

   Market share information may be found at www.sbdcnet.org, or go to your local library where you can get access to Reference USA, Consumer Affairs USA, and Gale's eReference resources, including Market Share Reporter (MSR) and the Business & Company Resource Center. Use Google Maps to search for competitors based on industry-related keywords for your target market. This will show you where most of your competitors are located. Visit at least 25 of your competitors' websites within the county (and surrounding counties or larger territory) that your business will serve.

3. Rank each of your competitors based on typical competitive factors. Evaluate the factors based on importance to the customer. Then rank your business. (See competition analysis template)

   Use the competition analysis template to complete this section.

4. What do the most successful competitors do to drive sales?

   Speak with (and meet with, if possible) the competitors outside of your market, as they can be an excellent resource for your business. Business owners love to help other business owners within their industry provided you are not considered to be a direct competitor.

5. How did you find your list of competitors?

   Write down how you found your competition. You can find your competition on websites, association sites, Google Maps, advertisements in magazines or newspapers, signs on the road, billboards, conferences, Facebook, email newsletters, tradeshows, word of mouth, radio, TV, etc. This will give you ideas for how you want to advertise your business.

Products and Services

1. List the products and services that your company sells and their functions.
2. How are your products and services impacted by technology changes?
3. How do you ensure consistent quality in your products and services?
4. How do your products compare to your competitors' products?
5. How do you manage your inventory levels to generate the highest profit?
6. Who are your major suppliers and vendors? What credit terms do your suppliers offer you? Why do you purchase from your existing suppliers? How long have you purchased from them?
7. How long does it take you to make, produce, or obtain the product for sale?
8. What types of warranties do you offer with your products and services? How often are warranties claimed by customers?

Sales and Marketing Plan

1. How many repeat (regular) customers does the business sell to? How often do your customers purchase products and services?
2. What customers represent more than 10% of your sales?
3. How many products do you (expect to) sell on a monthly basis? *Complete the Products and Services Revenue Calculator to estimate sales revenue to support your financial projections. This can be downloaded from www.ApprovedBook.com.*
4. What is the history of price increases?
5. Have unit sales increased or decreased in the last year? Last two years? Why?
6. How do you currently sell your products and services? (Door to door, storefront, phone, fax, Internet, catalog, etc.)
7. How do you price your products and services?
8. Are all sales made with cash upon sale or do you collect payment after providing your products or services?
9. What is the sales process from initial call to collection?
10. Do you offer any types of discounts or coupons?
11. What is your unique selling proposition (USP)? Why do your customers buy from you versus your competitors? (Refer to the competition analysis template previously completed)
12. How do you want your company to be viewed by your customers?
13. What are your marketing strategies online and offline? What is the monthly cost? (Website, email, newsletters, online advertisements, Facebook, Twitter, catalogs, TV, radio, fliers, cold calls, referral fees, etc.)
14. What type of advertising is most effective for generating leads and driving sales? Why?
15. Is your company a member of or affiliated with any trade organizations and associations? Provide details. How much do they cost? How do you participate?

Management and Organization Plan

1. Who are the managers and key employees of the company and what are their responsibilities?
2. How many non-management employees work for the company?
3. How are the existing company owners compensated? (Salary, bonus, car allowance, perks)
4. Does the company outsource services? (Contract labor, accounting, payroll)
5. What positions need to be filled? What will the responsibilities be? What will be the salary for each position?
6. Who are your board members, advisors, and consultants that influence the management of the company? List their names, roles with your company, and compensation. (Attorneys, accountants, marketing consultants, management consultants, etc.)
7. Do you require your employees to have any special training?
8. How do wages compare with the competition?

Operations Plan

1. What are the benefits of the company location? (Proximity to target market, access, lease rates, etc.)
2. What are the business hours of operation?
3. How many customers can the business serve on a daily basis? What is your maximum capacity? (You may be restricted by facility space, machinery output capacity, labor time, expertise, technology, etc.)
4. How does management control inventory and how does it relate to sales volume?
5. How does management control labor expenses related to sales volume?
6. How are discretionary expenses such as commissions, bonuses, and advertising managed?
7. What changes can be made to improve operations? How long would it take and what would be the cost?
8. How are accounts receivable and accounts payable managed?

9. How is working capital managed to cover accrued expenses such as payroll, loan interest, taxes, and bonuses?

Financial Plan

1. What were the company's sales as of the last fiscal year end? What were the company's sales as of the previous fiscal year end? Explain what impacted company sales from year to year.
2. What was the net income of the company for the last two fiscal years? Explain what impacted net income from year to year.
3. Have there been any one time (unusual) expenses in the last two fiscal years? What were these for, and why will they not occur in the future?
4. Describe your sales and net income since the last fiscal year end.
5. Is the company affiliated with any other businesses through common ownership or contracts? If so, how do these affiliated businesses impact cash flow?
6. Does the business have adequate working capital to support business growth?
7. What fixed asset (such as computers, vehicles, furniture, equipment, and real estate) expenditures are needed to maintain sales and/or grow the business? List assets desired to be purchased, anticipated purchase date, purpose, and cost.
8. Is cash on the balance sheet allocated for any specific use, such as new equipment?
9. What do you project sales to be for the next 12 months? Why? *Complete the financial projections template with financial projection assumptions to support your answer to this question. Templates can be downloaded from www.ApprovedBook.com.*
10. Do you project any one-time expenses in the future? What are they?

Executive Summary

1. Provide an overview of the company, including the company name, date the company was formed, and the current ownership. (See company summary)

2. Describe your target market and their product and service needs. (See target market analysis)

3. List the primary products and services sold by the company. (See products and services)

4. Describe your unique selling propositions. Why do customers buy from you versus your competition? (See sales and marketing)

5. How many customers can the business serve on a daily basis? What is the historical average of customers served daily? (See operations)

6. What were your sales for the last two years and year to date for the interim period? (See financial plan)

7. What trends in the industry (and/or market demand) have created opportunities for the company? (See industry analysis and target market)

8. What do you project sales to be for the next 12 months based on the opportunity? (See financial plan)

9. What is the estimated total project cost regardless of funding source (equity or debt)? (See application form: sources and uses of funds)

10. Why are you requesting financing for the business?

Appendices

The appendices are at the back of the business plan. This is where you will attach additional information that is relevant to the information discussed in the Business Plan Questionnaire. Include the following items:

1. Financial Projections
2. Products and Service Brochures, Fliers, Lists
3. Product Pictures
4. Feasibility Analysis
5. Market Studies
6. Relevant Articles
7. Vendor Contracts
8. Licenses, Permits, Patents
9. Letters of Reference

10. Résumés of Key Managers
11. Legal Documents

PART FIVE
THE SBA LOAN APPLICATION

Application errors are common. While most of the questions on an application are self-explanatory, many of the questions can be misunderstood, and it is easy to complete applications incorrectly. It is also common for applications to be submitted without supporting documentation or for the application information to slowly trickle into a lender. All of this causes processing delays, inaccurate underwriting submissions, and loan declines, all of which can be avoided. Another issue with incomplete application packages is that the start date for underwriting is continually delayed, taking second place to other complete applications submitted between the date your first application document was originally submitted and the date that your last application document is submitted. A third problem is that many lenders will just decline incomplete/incorrect applications because of the amount of time it takes to educate borrowers on how to provide the complete information. It can also be difficult to get a timely response from SBA professionals about application questions.

It is not your fault that you are not sure how to accurately complete and submit a business loan application. It is unlikely that you have made a career of knowing exactly how to apply for a business loan. Many of the application questions are confusing. Your business is successful because you are an expert at your business, not lending.

To address this common issue of incomplete and inaccurate loan application submissions, application templates have been developed that collect all of the information requested by an SBA lender to submit a complete file to underwriting. This collection of application templates is called the SBA application package. Part Five is a comprehensive manual including the template forms and detailed instructions on how to complete each of the application forms accurately. By following the information provided in this Part, you will be able to provide any lender with a complete and accurate application and it will be presented in such a way that your loan request will be expedited through the underwriting process.

The enclosed application templates were developed based on information collected from several of the top SBA lenders in the country. While application forms may differ slightly, the enclosed application templates request the identical information and can be used by any SBA lender as a replacement for the majority of their forms. Lenders are accustomed to accepting third-party forms and attachments provided that their application forms are signed with "see attached" written on them. In addition, the application templates have been designed to make sure that critical eligibility questions are asked to expedite processing.

The SBA application package is composed of 12 documents. The 12 templates provide the lender with specific information about the business, the owners, and the loan request necessary for underwriting purposes. These 12 documents are a document checklist, application summary template, sources and uses template, business debt schedule template, 4506-T template, business information template, projections template, personal financial statement template, personal income and expense template, statement of personal history template, résumé template, and credit authorization.

When completing the application pages, do your best to complete each of the forms in their entirety. Use this Part as a reference guide for your application questions. If you have a question about the enclosed application template forms or any lender specific application forms, it is likely that the clarification that you need is in this Part. Just match the question to the corresponding instructions. All template forms are available for download from www.ApprovedBook.com.

CHAPTER 11

THE SBA LOAN APPLICATION CHECKLIST

The application checklist is typically a coversheet for the application. It will be a general list of all of the documents that you will need to provide to the SBA lender for the lender to evaluate and underwrite your loan request. During the evaluation, the lender will determine his/her comfort with your business loan request and if he/she believes that the lender's credit committee will approve your request.

Prior to receiving the lender's checklist, the lender is likely to have a short introductory conversation with you to understand your request. The SBA lender will then send you a customized checklist detailing the items that you will need to prepare for a complete submission of your application. It is critical that every item requested by the lender be submitted as instructed. Most lenders will continue to send you the checklist on a weekly basis until the application package is complete. Most lenders will not begin analyzing the application package until all items have been received. This is due to the fact that each of the checklist items affect the other checklist items in the underwriting process. If something is missing and entered at a later date, the application profile continues to change, and it takes much longer to analyze an application that is amended multiple times.

Highlight the sections of the checklist that are applicable to your loan request.

SBA Loan Application Checklist

COMPANY INFORMATION:
① _____

BUSINESS APPLICATION AND PROJECT INFORMATION

Needed Completed
- ☐ ☐ ② Business Loan Application Summary (**form enclosed**)
- ☐ ☐ ③ Sources and Uses Worksheet - Project Cost Worksheet (**form enclosed**)

BUSINESS FINANCIAL INFORMATION (for applicant business or business being acquired, as applicable)

Needed Completed
- ☐ ☐ ④ Three (3) years of federal business tax returns for the applicant business
- ☐ ☐ ⑤ Current YTD Interim Financials - Balance Sheet, Profit and Loss, and AR/AP agings (dated within 60 days)
- ☐ ☐ ⑥ Business Debt Schedule (matching date & amount on current balance sheet) (**form enclosed**)
- ☐ ☐ ⑦ 4506-T Request for transcript of federal tax returns - signature only (**form enclosed**)
- ☐ ☐ ⑧ Business Information and History Form (**form enclosed**)
- ☐ ☐ ⑨ Financial Projections with Assumptions (monthly for first year, annualized for second year) (**form enclosed**)
- ☐ ☐ ⑩ Entity Documents: Corporation - Articles of Inc. & Bylaws; Partnership - Partnership Agreement (with exhibits); LLC - Articles of Organization Form and Operating Agreement; Trust - Trust Agreement and all exhibits
- ☐ ☐ ⑪ Lease Agreement (current or proposed for facility to be occupied)

AFFILIATED BUSINESS INFORMATION (ownership in other businesses - required for all 20%+ owners of applicant bus.)

Needed Completed
- ☐ ☐ ⑫ Three (3) years of federal business tax returns (include all schedules)
- ☐ ☐ ⑬ Current (dated within 60 days) Interim Financials - Balance Sheet, Profit and Loss, and AR/AP agings
- ☐ ☐ ⑭ Business Debt Schedule (matching date & amount on current balance sheet) (**form enclosed**)
- ☐ ☐ ⑮ 4506-T Request for transcript of federal tax returns - signature only (**form enclosed**)

PERSONAL FINANCIAL INFORMATION (required for all 20%+ owners of applicant business)

Needed Completed
- ☐ ☐ ⑯ Three (3) years of federal and state personal tax returns (include all schedles)
- ☐ ☐ ⑰ 4506-T Request for transcript of federal tax returns - signature only (**form enclosed**)
- ☐ ☐ ⑱ Personal Financial Statement - SBA form 413; signed by applicant and spouse (**form enclosed**)
- ☐ ☐ ⑲ Personal Income and Expense Form (**form enclosed**)
- ☐ ☐ ⑳ Statement of Personal History - SBA form 912 (**form enclosed**)
- ☐ ☐ ㉑ Management Resume (**form enclosed**)
- ☐ ☐ ㉒ Legible copy of State Driver's License, Passport, ID or Alien registration Card (if not U.S. Citizen)
- ☐ ☐ ㉓ Credit Authorization (**form inclosed**)

PROJECT SPECIFIC INFORMATION (include as applicable)

Needed Completed
- ☐ ☐ ㉔ Real Estate Purchase: purchase contract or letter of intent, property information, past/most recent appraisal and environmental reports, if available. Copy of earnest money check
- ☐ ☐ ㉕ Business Acquisition: purchase contract or letter of intent, 4506T signed by seller
- ☐ ☐ ㉖ Debt Refinance: copy of notes to be refinanced and recent loan statement
- ☐ ☐ ㉗ Start-Up Business: business plan & projected income statement: monthly for first year, quarterly for second year
- ☐ ☐ ㉘ Construction Project: contractor bids/estimate with construction schedule; contract with plans & specs (ideally)
- ☐ ☐ ㉙ Equipment Purchase: copy of purchase order/invoice or description of equipment to be purchased with an estimate of the cost.
- ☐ ☐ ㉚ Franchise: franchise agreement, franchise offering circular, & FTC franchise disclosure statement

- ☐ ☐ ㉛ _____
- ☐ ☐ _____
- ☐ ☐ _____
- ☐ ☐ _____
- ☐ ☐ _____

The SBA Loan Application Checklist pictured on the opposite page was developed to include at least 95% of the items that you will need to provide to achieve loan approval. Depending on the complexity of your application, additional documentation may be required. This checklist is great because the lender can quickly check the items that you will need to submit based on your loan request and then you can check off the items as they are submitted.

1. In the top right of the page, there is a section for company information. This is where you will list the company name, primary contact, and primary contact's phone number.

Business Application

2. The business loan application summary* is the second page of the SBA application package. This form summarizes the applicant business and the loan request.

3. The sources and uses worksheet* is page three of the SBA application package. The form details all of the intended uses of the funding request. It also identifies the sources of the money, including loans and money to be injected into the transaction.

Business Financial Information

4. Three years of federal business tax returns are required for the applicant business. If the business has been in existence for less than three years, provide the tax returns for the years it has existed.

5. Current year-to-date (YTD) interim financials are required for the applicant business. The interim financials should be printed as of a month end date and within 60 days of the application date (30 days is better). The YTD income statement (profit and loss statement) should represent the income and expenses of the business starting from the first day of the company's fiscal year (commonly January 1) through the most recent month end date. The interim period should be no more than one full year. The balance sheet should be generated based on the assets and liabilities of the company as of the most recent month end date. If

your accounting is prepared on an accrual basis (rather than on a cash basis), you will have additional reports called "aging reports." You will know if your financial statements are prepared on an accrual basis if you see "accounts receivable" listed in the asset section of your balance sheet and "accounts payable" listed in the liability section of your balance sheet. The aging reports, better known as accounts receivable (A/R) and accounts payable (A/P) should be printed as of the most recent month end date to match the month end date of the income statement and balance sheet. The aging report balances should match the balances represented on the balance sheet.

6. The business debt schedule* is the fourth page of the SBA application package. This schedule represents all of the debt for which the applicant business is responsible. Business debt may include auto loans, real estate loans, equipment loans, lines of credit, and other debts paid for the business.

7. The IRS Form 4506-T* is pages five and six of the SBA application package. The 4506-T is required by the SBA to authenticate tax return information submitted with the application and to prevent fraud.

8. The business information and history* form is the seventh page of the SBA application package. This form provides the lender with a quick summary of your business—an overview of the past, present, and future of the company.

9. The financial projections* form is the eighth page of the SBA application package. This form is required for all start-up businesses, changes of ownership, or where historical cash flow does not support the requested loan amount. This form is commonly required in situations where the financing will enable a company to grow.

10. Entity documents are the legal documents that were created to establish your company, file taxes, employ staff, and open bank accounts. Your attorney and accountant will typically keep copies of these. If your business was established as a corporation, articles of incorporation, bylaws, and tax ID number (EIN) are required in addition to any amendments, exhibits, or trade name filings. If

your business was established as a partnership, your partnership agreement (operating agreement) and EIN are required in addition to any amendments, exhibits, or trade name filings. If your business was established as a limited liability company (LLC), articles of organization (certificate of organization), operating agreement, and EIN are required in addition to any amendments, exhibits, or trade name filings. If your business was established as a trust, your trust agreement and all exhibits are required. If your business is operating as a sole proprietorship, copy of any trade name (fictitious/assumed name) filing is required.

11. The lease agreement is the lease for the space that your business occupies to conduct business. If your business currently owns the real estate occupied by the business, a lease may not be applicable. If your business will lease space as a result of the SBA loan, the new lease is required.

Affiliated Business Information

12. Three years of federal business tax returns are required for all other businesses considered to be affiliates. Affiliate businesses are other businesses (not the applicant business) in which the applicant borrowers have at least a 20% interest. All available tax returns are required if the affiliate business has been in existence for less than three years.

13. Current interim (YTF) financials are required for all affiliate businesses. The interim financials should be printed with the same month end date as the applicant business interim financial statements were printed. For additional information about interim financial statements, see number five.

14. A business debt schedule* is required for each affiliate business. Prepare a separate business debt schedule for each affiliate business including those with no debt.

15. A 4506-T* form is required for each affiliate business. Prepare a separate IRS Form 4506-T for each of these businesses based on the instructions provided in the IRS Form 4506-T section of this Part.

Personal Financial Information

16. Three years of federal and state personal tax returns are required for all 20% or greater owners of the applicant business. Make sure to include all schedules and exhibits of the personal tax return including W-2s.

17. A 4506-T* form is required for all applicant borrowers that will have at least a 20% ownership interest in the applicant business.

18. The personal financial statement* (SBA Form 413) includes pages nine through 13 of the SBA loan application package. SBA Form 413 is required to be submitted by all applicant borrowers that will have at least a 20% ownership interest in the applicant business. If joint returns are filed with a spouse, personal financial statements are to include financial information on both spouses and the statements are to be signed by both spouses.

19. The personal income and expense* form is page 14 of the SBA application package. This form provides a summary of your family's sources of income and expense.

20. The statement of personal history* (SBA Form 912) is page 15 and 16 of the SBA application package. This form is required by all business loan applicants with at least a 20% ownership interest.

21. The management résumé* is page 17 and 18 of the SBA application package. The management résumé is to be completed by all applicants with at least a 20% ownership interest.

22. For legible copy of ID card, provide a clear (color is possible) copy of your unexpired state-issued driver's license. If a driver's license is not available, provide a copy of your government-issued passport, passport card, or other US government-issued ID card. If any 20% or greater owner is not a US citizen but has permanent US resident status, a copy of the permanent resident card is required in addition to the US identification card.

23. The credit authorization* is page 19 (last page) of the SBA application package. The credit authorization is a sample credit authorization form required to be completed by all applicants with at least a 20% ownership interest.

Project Specific Information

24. If your transaction involves a <u>real estate purchase</u>, additional documentation including a fully executed purchase contract, property details such as that provided by the listing agent, and copy of any earnest money deposits will be required. Providing previously prepared appraisals and environmental reports may expedite processing.

25. If your transaction involves a <u>business acquisition</u>, additional documentation including a fully executed purchase contract, business details such as that provided by the listing agent or seller, and a copy of any earnest money deposits will be required. The seller is responsible for providing #4 (business tax returns), #5 (interim financials), and #7 (IRS Form 4506-T) described above.

26. For a transaction involving <u>debt refinance</u>, additional documentation, including a copy of the note (loan agreement) and a recent loan statement evidencing payment amount and the current balance, will be required. For lease obligations to be refinanced such as an equipment lease, a copy of the lease agreement and current lease statement (if available) will be required.

27. For a transaction involving a <u>start-up business</u> (business in existence for less than two years), a business plan with two years of projections is required. For information on how to complete a simple SBA loan friendly business plan, see Part Four, the business plan questionnaire.

28. For a transaction involving <u>construction</u>, contractor bids (estimates) with a construction schedule is the minimum requirement for SBA loan approval. Most SBA lenders require an executed construction contract with plans and specifications. Nailing down all soft and hard construction costs prior to application dramatically reduces time delays and construction funding issues.

29. For a transaction involving <u>equipment purchases</u>, a copy of the purchase order/invoice will be requested. In many cases, an estimate of the cost with description of the equipment, such as from a catalog, is acceptable.

30. If the transaction involves a <u>franchise</u> business, the executed franchise agreement, franchise offering circular, and FTC franchise disclosure

statement are required. The SBA lender may require additional documentation depending on the franchise and franchise eligibility.

31. The spaces at the bottom are for additional documents that may be requested by the SBA lender due to unique circumstances of your particular SBA loan request.

* Detailed instructions for how to complete each of the application forms are included in this Part.

CHAPTER 12

BUSINESS LOAN APPLICATION SUMMARY

The Business Loan Application Summary is typically the first page after the checklist. This is where you will provide general information about the company and the applicant owners. Listed below are the instructions for how to complete the form, with corresponding numbers for easy reference.

From the top of the business loan application summary page, complete the form as follows:

Business Information
1. <u>Company name</u> is the legal name under which the operating company transacts business. Entity names of a company operating for the sole purpose of holding real estate should be listed in section #12.
2. <u>Date established</u>: List the date the company was originally established. Date should be listed in mm/dd/yyyy format.
3. <u>Type of business</u>: Provide a high-level industry category such as metal manufacturer or childcare provider. If you provide a wide variety of

Business Loan Application Summary

BUSINESS INFORMATION

COMPANY NAME: ①   DATE ESTABLISHED: ②

TYPE OF BUSINESS: ③   TAX ID #: ④   DUNS #: ⑤

PHYSICAL ADDRESS: ⑥   NUMBER OF EMPLOYEES NOW: ⑦

CITY: STATE: ZIP: NUMBER OF EMPLOYEES AFTER LOAN: ⑧

BUSINESS PHONE: ⑨   BUSINESS WEBSITE: ⑩

⑪ TYPE OF BUSINESS ENTITY: ☐ S CORP. ☐ C COR. ☐ PARTNERSHIP ☐ LP ☐ LLP ☐ LLC ☐ TRUST ☐ SOLE PROP. ☐ OTHER ⑪

IF REAL ESTATE WILL BE HELD IN A SEPARATE ENTITY, WHAT IS THE ENTITY NAME ⑫

⑬ PRIMARY APPLICATION CONTACT: (W) PHONE: MOBILE PHONE:

PRIMARY CONTACT EMAIL:

BUSINESS OWNERSHIP INFORMATION

⑭	OWNERS' NAMES	TITLE	RESPONSIBILITIES	Ownership %
1				
2				
3				
4				

AFFILIATE BUSINESS INFORMATION (ownership by any 20%+ owners in other businesses)

⑮	AFFILIATE BUSINESS NAME	TYPE OF BUSINESS	OWNER NAME	Ownership %
1				
2				
3				
4				
5				

ADDITIONAL BUSINESS INFORMATION

⑯ Has the company or any owner of the company ever been involved in a bankruptcy or insolvency proceeding? ⑯ ○ Yes ○ No

⑰ Is the company or any principal of the company involved in any lawsuits? ⑰ ○ Yes ○ No

⑱ Does the company owe any taxes (including real estate or payroll) for years prior to the current year? ⑱ ○ Yes ○ No

LOAN REQUEST INFORMATION

What is the purpose of the loan request?

⑲

PROFESSIONAL BUSINESS ADVISOR CONTACT INFORMATION

⑳ ACCOUNTANT/CPA: (W) PHONE: MOBILE PHONE:

㉑ ATTORNEY: (W) PHONE: MOBILE PHONE:

㉒ INSURANCE AGENT: (W) PHONE: MOBILE PHONE:

㉓ REAL ESTATE BROKER: (W) PHONE: MOBILE PHONE:

㉔

products and services, pick the industry that represents the majority of the business's income.

4. Tax ID (or EIN): Enter the number that was issued by the IRS when the company's legal entity was established.

5. DUNS number: The DUNS number, is basically a Social Security number for your business that is location specific. Getting a DUNS number is important as you will use it to establish a credit score for your company. To get a free DUNS number, go to https://iupdate.dnb.com and click on "get a DUNS number". Make sure to choose "yes" to the question about government funding so that the DUNS number is free.

6. Physical address: Make sure to list your business's physical address even if your mailing address is different. If you have several locations, list the primary physical address or corporate headquarters.

7. Number of employees now: List the total number of employees including owners that work at the company as of the date of the application.

8. Number of employees after loan: Provide a number of employees expected. This should be no fewer than the number of employees now since a major objective of SBA loans is to increase employment opportunities.

9. Business phone: List the business's primary phone number.

10. Business website: List the company's website or leave a blank if one does not exist.

11. Type of business entity: Check the entity type that corresponds with the company name listed in #1.

12. Real estate entity: If real estate is or will be owned by a separate legal entity (company), enter the real estate entity name here. This entity name will be different from the operating company listed in #1. Leave a blank if not applicable.

13. Primary application contact: Delegate one of the applicant owners to be the primary application contact. This is the person who the lender will ask the majority of the business-related questions. Provide his/her full name, direct phone number, cell phone number, and direct email

address. Having direct access to a primary point of contact streamlines the underwriting process.

Business Ownership Information

14. Business ownership information: List each of the business applicant owners' full names, title, high-level company responsibility, and ownership percentage. Attach an exhibit to provide the same information if there are more than four business owners.

Affiliate Business Information

15. Affiliate business information: List all other businesses in which any of the applicant owners (#14) have at least a 20% ownership interest. In addition to the affiliate company name, list the type of business, the name of the applicant owner, and his/her percentage of ownership. Attach a separate exhibit as needed.

Additional Business Information

16. If the company or any of the 20% or greater owners has ever filed for bankruptcy, check "yes" and provide a letter describing the circumstances that led to the bankruptcy.

17. If the company or any principal of the company is involved in a lawsuit (other than a car insurance claim), check "yes" and attach a written explanation describing the circumstances of the lawsuit and how the business will be impacted.

18. If the company is behind on taxes, provide a written explanation of why the company is behind and the negotiated repayment plan documentation.

Loan Request Information

19. Loan request information: Provide details for the purpose of the loan request. Specify how the loan proceeds will benefit the business.

Professional Business Advisor Contact Information

20. <u>Accountant/CPA</u>: Provide the contact information for the business's accountant, including full name, direct work phone number, and cell phone.

21. <u>Attorney</u>: Provide the contact information for the attorney who will represent you at closing and/or that helped you form your company's legal entity. Provide his/her full name, direct work phone number, and cell phone.

22. <u>Insurance agent</u>: Provide the contact information for your insurance agent that handles your business insurance. Provide his/her full name, direct work phone number, and cell phone.

23. <u>Real estate broker</u>: If there is a real estate broker representing the real estate or business purchase, provide the contact information for the broker, including full name, direct work phone number, and cell phone.

24. Use the space at the bottom of the form to provide additional contact information such as email addresses for those identified and other contact people who are involved in the transaction such as a loan broker, consultant, or seller.

CHAPTER 13

SOURCES AND USES OF FUNDS

The sources and uses of funds template is a snapshot of all money in and out of a transaction. "Sources of funds" represents all of the capital coming into the transaction including capital that you are going to borrow, capital that you will invest from personal resources, and capital that will be contributed from other sources such as investors, family, and friends. "Uses of funds" represents the total allocation of capital for the benefit of your business.

Prior to requesting financing, you will generate a list of how capital will be allocated. Once you know your capital requirements, you can then calculate how much financing you will request. For this reason, "uses of funds" is completed first. Don't get hung up on any line item. Just do your best to estimate how much money to allocate to each category even if it is zero. For undefined amounts such as construction, estimate on the high side. After submission of your loan application package, expect your lender to confirm allocations with you and make minor adjustments as necessary.

From the top of the "sources and uses of funds" template, complete the form as follows:

Sources and Uses of Funds

COMPANY NAME: _____ ①_____

USES OF FUNDS

Purchase/Refinance Land:	②
Purchase/Refinance Land & Building:	③
Construction - Ground Up / Expand Building:	④
Construction - Renovation/Leasehold Improvements:	⑤
Construction Soft Costs (Architect, Engineering/Permits, etc):	⑥
Business Acquisition (stock sale or asset sale):	⑦
Purchase Machinery and Equipment:	⑧
Purchase Inventory:	⑨
Purchase Furniture and Fixtures:	⑩
Refinance Existing Business Debt:	⑪
Refinance Existing SBA Loan:	⑫
Working Capital:	⑬
Closing Costs:	⑭
Other: ⑮	⑯

TOTAL PROJECT COST: ⑰ $0

SOURCE OF FUNDS

Borrower's Equity Contribution (down payment):*	⑱
Bank/SBA Loan Requested:	⑲
Other: _____ ⑳	㉑
Other: _____ ⑳	㉑

TOTAL SOURCES OF FUNDING: ㉒ $0

*Detail the source(s) of the downpayment:

㉓

1. <u>Company name</u>: Enter the legal name of which the operating company transacts business. For example, John's Painting Company, LLC.

Uses of Funds

2. <u>Purchase/refinance land</u>: Enter the total dollar amount allocated for the purchase (or refinance a loan secured by) unimproved/vacant land. If there is an existing building on the land, do not enter a dollar amount but go to #3. If not applicable, enter zero dollars.

3. <u>Purchase/refinance land and building</u>: Enter the total dollar amount allocated to purchase (or refinance a loan secured by) a building for your business. If real estate is not included in your financing request, enter zero dollars.

4. <u>Construction—ground up/expand building</u>: If your financing request will include construction and the construction *will* increase the amount of building space, enter the dollar amount to be spent on real estate construction. This construction expense should increase the value of the property. Enter zero dollars if not applicable.

5. <u>Construction—renovation/leasehold improvements</u>: Enter the dollar amount to be spent on renovation that *will not* increase the square footage of an existing building. This construction expense may or may not increase the value of the existing real estate. If capital will be used to transform a leased space into more usable space for your business, such as moving walls around, renovating a bathroom, or building a commercial kitchen, list the total construction estimate. Leased space is typically space that your company does not own, like a shopping center. This category may also be used for space in a building that your business *does* own but the interior improvements may not have a material impact on the appraised value of the building. For example, medical and veterinarian borrowers invest substantial capital toward leasehold improvements including special lighting, plumbing, electrical and other fixtures that generally do not materially impact the value of the building as a whole. If you move, the landlord may have to tear everything out to provide the next tenant with a vanilla shell

like you were initially provided. If no capital will be allocated to this section, leave it at zero dollars.

6. Construction soft costs: Enter the dollar amount allocated for construction soft costs. Soft costs are construction-related expenses that provide little benefit to the value of the property but are necessary for the construction project to commence. Examples of soft costs include permit fees, architect fees, and engineering fees. If you are not sure of the amount of construction soft costs or they are not applicable, leave this allocation at zero dollars.

7. Business acquisition: The purchase price of a business will typically include a variety of assets such as real estate, equipment, inventory, leasehold improvements, and intangible assets (e.g., goodwill). If the business acquisition price includes real estate and a value for the real estate has been included in the purchase contract, enter the value given for the real estate in #3 and the balance of the purchase price here at #7. If an allocation of assets is not specified in the purchase contract, enter the entire business acquisition price here. If funding a business acquisition is not applicable, leave this section at zero dollars.

8. Purchase machinery and equipment: If you will be acquiring any machinery or equipment as part of this transaction, enter the total cost of these items. If you have already acquired machinery or equipment and it was a recent acquisition (within the last six months), include this amount in the total for this category. Make sure to specify what will be acquired and what has already been acquired. Documentation will be necessary for any purchases previously made. Do not include any machinery and equipment that has been included in #7.

9. Purchase inventory: Enter the amount of capital allocated for the purchase of inventory. Inventory includes raw goods used to manufacture a finished product and finished products ready for sale. If inventory is not an intended use of capital, enter zero. Note that when your application is submitted for SBA approval, the amount you listed for inventory is likely to be included in the SBA's permanent working capital category.

Do not include an amount for inventory if it was previously accounted for in #7.

10. Purchase furniture and fixtures: Enter the amount of capital allocated for the purchase of furniture and fixtures. If furniture and fixtures are not an intended use of capital, enter zero. Do not include furniture and fixtures if they were accounted for in #7.

11. Refinance existing business debt: Enter the amount of capital allocated for the purpose of refinancing existing non-SBA business debt. Refinancing non-SBA business debt is a common use of SBA financing due to the advantages that SBA loans can provide over traditional business debt. Existing business debt may include debt for business real estate, equipment and machinery debt, partnership buyout debt, seller loans taken when the business was acquired, other debt used to finance goodwill, business lines of credit, leases, and business credit card debt. All business debt should be listed on the business debt schedule template discussed later in this Part. Personal debt used for business purposes can be refinanced as well, however, additional documentation will be required to determine eligibility. If capital has not been allocated for the purpose of debt refinance, enter zero dollars.

12. Refinance existing SBA loan: Enter the amount of capital allocated for the purpose of refinancing your business's existing SBA debt. If capital has not been allocated for the purpose of refinancing existing SBA debt, enter zero dollars.

13. Working capital: Working capital is one of the most common financing requests by business owners. In many cases, the purpose of the working capital actually falls into one of the previous categories. If additional capital is desired, enter the amount allocated for working capital. For start-up and expanding businesses, it is common to need working capital to support operating expenses until the business is generating adequate cash flow. This is discussed in the business plan projections section of Part Four. If working capital has not been allocated as a use of capital, enter zero dollars.

14. Closing costs: As discussed in Part Two, closing costs are calculated based on your unique set of circumstances, but they are highly regulated by the SBA to make sure the program is affordable. For this reason, it is recommended that the amount listed here remain at zero dollars. Once the loan request is submitted to the SBA lender, the lender will calculate this figure for you. Do note that once closing costs have been calculated, the total project cost detailed in #17 will increase.

15. Other (undefined uses of funds): If you are not sure which is the appropriate category to allocate your use of capital funds, enter the description of how the funds will be used in the space provided.

16. Other (dollar amount): Enter the dollar amount that is allocated toward the "other" use of funds described in #15.

17. Total project cost: The total project cost will auto-calculate in the form. This represents the total allocation of capital.

Source of Funds

18. Borrower's equity contribution (down payment): If you are unsure of the amount of equity injection that will be required by the SBA lender, enter zero dollars for equity injection. As discussed in Part Two, an equity injection is usually required, however, the dollar amount is usually less than what is required through non-SBA programs. The SBA lender will determine the amount of equity injection that will be needed.

19. Bank/SBA loan requested: Enter the amount of financing requested.

20. Other (undefined source of funds): Enter the alternative source of funding that is neither your equity injection nor bank/SBA financing. The most common alternative source of funding is seller financing.

21. Other (dollar amount): Enter the dollar amount provided by the alternative source.

22. Total sources of funding: The total source of funding represents the total of all sources. The "total sources of funding" is calculated by the form. The "total sources of funding" should match the "total uses of funds" as reported in #17. If #22 and #17 do not match, adjust #19 until they do.

23. <u>Detail the source(s) of the down payment</u>: Detail the source of #18. If you entered zero dollars for #18, enter your sources of down payment from which an equity injection could be drawn. Typical answers include business savings account, personal savings account, sale of marketable securities, 401(k) rollover, investments by minority shareholders, family members, etc.

Now that you have completed the sources and uses of funds form, print the completed form and put it in a three-ring binder with the other application pages.

CHAPTER 14

BUSINESS DEBT SCHEDULE

When applying for a business loan, the business debt schedule is one of the most important documents for a lender to evaluate. The business debt schedule provides the lender with a snapshot of all of the liabilities of a business. The lender will use this information to determine if the cash flow of the business can support additional debt or if existing debt can be refinanced on more favorable terms.

The business debt schedule, often simply called a "debt schedule," is a detailed list of all of a company's liabilities that are summarized on its balance sheet. Information included on the business debt schedule will include the business name, date (should match the date of the balance sheet), list of loans and lines of credit with corresponding bank names, original balances, current balances, interest rates, collateral, monthly payment amounts, and maturity dates. A sample template has been enclosed. With a few exceptions, all of the information can be completed from the monthly statements provided by the lenders (creditors).

While personal credit reports are fairly accurate, business credit reports usually fail to report all of a business's debt obligations. A properly completed business debt schedule makes it simple for the business owner and the lender to know exactly the monthly debt obligations of the business. The schedule also provides an overview for the range of interest rates charged, upcoming maturities or balloons, prepayment penalties, and potential refinancing opportunities. Some of my best customers update a form like this on a monthly basis so they always know where they stand with their business debt. It's also a lot easier to keep a business debt schedule accurate and current unlike a balance sheet that frequently is incomprehensible to business owners.

To determine an applicant's capacity to borrow money, the information presented on the business debt schedule is going to be compared with the profitability of the applicant company as presented on the income (profit and loss) statement of the company.

The business debt schedule will list a variety of types of debt including mortgage debt, term debt, and lines of credit. Mortgage debt is simply a loan secured by real estate. The real estate could be residential, commercial, or unimproved or improved land that is owned by the applicant business. Term debt is a broad category covering all other nonrevolving debt. This may include equipment loans, auto loans, goodwill loans, partnership buyout loans, leasehold improvements loans, and the like. Operating leases such as leases of autos and equipment are not to be listed as loans on the business debt schedule. It is common for a business owner to want to add leased equipment (for example, printers) and autos on the business debt schedule; however, this is only correct if it is a capital lease where ownership is transferred to the company at no or a nominal cost at the end of the lease term.

Lines of credit (LOC) are the third category of debt listed on a business debt schedule. It is important for you and the bank to understand the terms of your LOC. The original amount should be the maximum amount that can be borrowed on the LOC. The current balance is the present debt as of the date of the business debt schedule. The payment is likely to be the current balance times the interest rate divided by 12. For example, if a company has an LOC with a $10,000 balance at 6%, the monthly interest only payment will be $50 ($10,000 x 6% / 12 = $50). The annual interest paid would be $600, with monthly interest payments of $50. Business credit cards should also be listed on the business debt schedule, with corresponding information obtained from statements or from online access. In all cases, payment information obtained directly from the issuing creditor is going to be of greatest value. If payment amounts are not listed, bankers will have to make assumptions, and they usually estimate high to be conservative. For credit cards, bankers generally go with 3% of the outstanding balance as this will usually account for interest and some principal reduction, which is normally required.

To avoid double counting debt obligations, debts listed on the business debt schedule will be matched with any debts listed on business and personal credit reports. Identifying all debts that are personally guaranteed will avoid duplication. For example, the interest on business debts, including credit cards, will be expensed by the business on the income statement (profit and loss statement) of the company. If these debts are not identified and also reported on the personal credit report, the interest expense will be deducted again during the personal income and expense analysis, resulting in double counting. It is never in a borrower's interest for a bank to calculate that you have more monthly obligations than you actually do, so clearly identify all personal and business debt obligations.

All debt that is paid for by the business should be listed on the business debt schedule.

1. Company name: List only one company name. A separate business debt schedule should be completed for each company. Only debt paid for by this company should be listed.

2. As of month end date: List the date to match the month end date of the interim financial statements. For instance, if you submit March 31 financial statements, the business debt schedule date should reflect March 31. The total debt listed on the March 31 balance sheet should match the total debt listed on the business debt schedule.

Business Debt Obligations

3. Creditor name: Enter the finance company or lender to which the company owes the debt.

Business Debt Schedule (include leases)

Company Name: _____ (1)

As of Month End Date: _____ (2)
(match interim statements)

Business Debt Obligations

Creditor Name / Account Number	Original Date	Original Amount	Present Balance	Interest Rate	Monthly Payment	Maturity Date	Collateral/Security Address	Use of Funds/ Loan Purpose	SBA Debt? Refinance?
(3) (4)	(5)	(6)	(7)	(8)	(9)	(10)	(11) (12)	(13)	(14) (15) + ( ) ▸ (16)
									+ ( ) ▸
									+ ( ) ▸
									+ ( ) ▸
TOTAL BALANCE:			(17)		TOTAL: (18)				

Business Debt Obligations

Lessor Name (landlord/Finance Co.)	Lease/Account Number	Lease Start Date	Expiration Date	Monthly Payment	Current Balance	Leased Property Description, Collateral and Other Information	Use of Lease/ Lease Purpose	Refinance?
(19)	(20)	(21)	(22)	(23)	(24)	(25)	(26)	(27) + ( ) + ( ) ▸ (28)
	Totals:			(29)	(30)			

Applicant Name: _____ (31)

Applicant Signature: _____ (32)

Date: _____ (33)

Page 1 of 1

4. Account number: List the complete loan number so that it can be matched with loan statements.

5. Original date: List the date on which the loan was originally loaned to the business by the creditor. Enter the date in mm/dd/yyyy format.

6. Original amount: List the original loan amount loaned to the business. For lines of credit, list the line of credit limit. For example, if you have a $50,000 line of credit and only have a balance of $10,000, list $50,000 as the original balance.

7. Present balance: List the balance as of the date listed at the top of the form. Attaching a loan statement matching the date listed at the top of the form will be appreciated by the lender.

8. Interest rate: Enter the current interest rate. Many loans are tied to either adjustable interest rates or interest rates that may be increased or decreased during the term of the loan. The current interest rate should be listed on your loan statement.

9. Monthly payment: Enter the minimum required payment amount. Do not list an amount greater than the minimum payment even if you typically pay a larger amount to accelerate principal reduction.

10. Maturity date: Enter the date when the loan comes due. It is common for commercial loans to have a repayment term that is shorter than the amortization period on which the payments are based. Enter the date in mm/dd/yyyy format.

11. Collateral/security: List the assets that secure the loan. This is typically either all business assets or specific assets such as equipment, real estate, or accounts receivable.

12. (Collateral) address: List the address where the collateral is located.

13. Use of funds: List the purpose of the loan. What did the loan enable the business to acquire? Typical answers are working capital, to purchase real estate, to purchase equipment, etc.

14. SBA debt: Enter "yes" if the loan is an SBA loan. "Yes" or "no" can also be selected from the drop-down box.

15. Refinance: If you intend to refinance this loan as part of your financing request, enter "yes." You can also choose "yes" or "no" from the drop-down box.

16. At the end of each row is a plus and minus sign. If you need additional rows to enter all of your business debts, press the plus sign and an additional row will be added. If you want to delete a row, you can press the minus sign and after a confirmation message, you can delete a row including the information listed in the row.

17. Total balance: The dollar figure generated next to total balance should represent the total balance that this business owes to its creditors.

18. Total: The total monthly payment should represent the total of all minimum payments of all this business's debts as of the date listed at the top of the form.

Business Lease Obligations

19. Lessor name: Enter the name of the person or company to which monthly lease payments are made. An example of lessor could be your landlord for the space occupied by the business. Another example could be a finance company that is financing equipment through a lease purchase.

20. Lease account number: List the complete account number (as applicable) for your lease. If you have a lease agreement, attach it to this form.

21. Lease start date: List the date on which the lease was originally made regardless of the number of extensions. Enter the date in mm/dd/yyyy format.

22. Lease expiration date: List the current lease expiration date. Enter the date in mm/dd/yyyy format. For options to renew, see #25.

23. Monthly payment: List the dollar amount that is paid on a monthly basis to the landlord.

24. Current balance: Enter the amount due to completely satisfy the lease debt. For a lease, this is likely to be the total of all remaining payments.

25. Leased property description, collateral, and other information: Enter information about the type of lease and how it is secured. For other information, enter if there are lease extension options available to you

and what those are, such as "2x5 year extension." Also list if additional payments such as taxes or HOA fees are required as part of the lease.

26. <u>Use of lease</u>: Enter the purpose of the lease. Typical lease purposes include office space or equipment.

27. <u>Refinance</u>: If you intend to pay off the lease as part of your financing request, enter "yes." You can also choose "yes" or "no" from the drop-down box.

28. If you need additional rows to enter all of your business's leases, press the plus sign and an additional row will be added. If you want to delete a row, press the minus sign and after a confirmation message, you can delete a row, including any information listed in the row.

29. <u>Total (monthly payment)</u>: The total monthly payment should represent the total lease payment paid on a monthly basis.

30. <u>Total (current balance)</u>: The number generated for total current balance should represent the total balance due on existing leases as of the date of the form.

31. <u>Applicant name</u>: List an owner's name who is authorized to sign on behalf of the company.

32. <u>Applicant signature</u>: The person listed in #31 should sign the form.

33. <u>Date</u>: The applicant is to date the form as of the date of completion. Enter the date in mm/dd/yyyy format.

CHAPTER 15

IRS FORM 4506-T

The purpose of IRS Form 4506-T is to allow a lender to verify that a business files business tax returns with the IRS and that these returns provided as part of the application agree with the business tax returns that were filed with the IRS. This protects the applicant borrower, the SBA lender, and the SBA from fraud usually attempted to inflate the actual value of a company.

The lender will verify business tax returns for all years, up to three years, that the business has been in operation. If the business is a start-up for which no taxes have been required to be filed with the IRS, verification will not be required. On occasion, a business owner will file an amended business tax return with the IRS to replace a previously filed return. If the business owner fails to inform the SBA lender, the business tax return numbers may not match up with the IRS numbers. If there is a discrepancy, the discrepancy will be investigated and must be corrected for the loan request to be processed.

TIP: If an extension has been filed for the most recent fiscal year, make sure to submit a copy of the tax return extension and a copy of the canceled check evidencing payment of the estimated taxes.

Form **4506-T**	**Request for Transcript of Tax Return**	
(Rev. September 2013) Department of the Treasury Internal Revenue Service	▶ Request may be rejected if the form is incomplete or illegible.	OMB No. 1545-1872

Tip. Use Form 4506-T to order a transcript or other return information free of charge. See the product list below. You can quickly request transcripts by using our automated self-help service tools. Please visit us at IRS.gov and click on "Order a Return or Account Transcript" or call 1-800-908-9946. If you need a copy of your return, use **Form 4506, Request for Copy of Tax Return.** There is a fee to get a copy of your return.

1a Name shown on tax return. If a joint return, enter the name shown first.
(1)

1b First social security number on tax return, individual taxpayer identification number, or employer identification number (see instructions)
(2)

2a If a joint return, enter spouse's name shown on tax return.
(3)

2b Second social security number or individual taxpayer identification number if joint tax return
(4)

3 Current name, address (including apt., room, or suite no.), city, state, and ZIP code (see instructions)
(5)

4 Previous address shown on the last return filed if different from line 3 (see instructions)
(6)

5 If the transcript or tax information is to be mailed to a third party (such as a mortgage company), enter the third party's name, address, and telephone number.
(7)

Caution. If the tax transcript is being mailed to a third party, ensure that you have filled in lines 6 through 9 before signing. Sign and date the form once you have filled in these lines. Completing these steps helps to protect your privacy. Once the IRS discloses your tax transcript to the third party listed on line 5, the IRS has no control over what the third party does with the information. If you would like to limit the third party's authority to disclose your transcript information, you can specify this limitation in your written agreement with the third party.

6 **Transcript requested.** Enter the tax form number here (1040, 1065, 1120, etc.) and check the appropriate box below. Enter only one tax form number per request. ▶

(8)

a **Return Transcript,** which includes most of the line items of a tax return as filed with the IRS. A tax return transcript does not reflect changes made to the account after the return is processed. Transcripts are only available for the following returns: Form 1040 series, Form 1065, Form 1120, Form 1120A, Form 1120H, Form 1120L, and Form 1120S. Return transcripts are available for the current year and returns processed during the prior 3 processing years. Most requests will be processed within 10 business days . . . . . . ☐

b **Account Transcript,** which contains information on the financial status of the account, such as payments made on the account, penalty assessments, and adjustments made by you or the IRS after the return was filed. Return information is limited to items such as tax liability and estimated tax payments. Account transcripts are available for most returns. Most requests will be processed within 10 business days . ☐

c **Record of Account,** which provides the most detailed information as it is a combination of the Return Transcript and the Account Transcript. Available for current year and 3 prior tax years. Most requests will be processed within 10 business days . . . . ☐

7 **Verification of Nonfiling,** which is proof from the IRS that you **did not** file a return for the year. Current year requests are only available after June 15th. There are no availability restrictions on prior year requests. Most requests will be processed within 10 business days . . ☐

8 **Form W-2, Form 1099 series, Form 1098 series, or Form 5498 series transcript.** The IRS can provide a transcript that includes data from these information returns. State or local information is not included with the Form W-2 information. The IRS may be able to provide this transcript information for up to 10 years. Information for the current year is generally not available until the year after it is filed with the IRS. For example, W-2 information for 2011, filed in 2012, will likely not be available from the IRS until 2013. If you need W-2 information for retirement purposes, you should contact the Social Security Administration at 1-800-772-1213. Most requests will be processed within 10 business days . ☐

Caution. If you need a copy of Form W-2 or Form 1099, you should first contact the payer. To get a copy of the Form W-2 or Form 1099 filed with your return, you must use Form 4506 and request a copy of your return, which includes all attachments.

9 **Year or period requested.** Enter the ending date of the year or period, using the mm/dd/yyyy format. If you are requesting more than four years or periods, you must attach another Form 4506-T. For requests relating to quarterly tax returns, such as Form 941, you must enter each quarter or tax period separately.
(9)

Check this box if you have notified the IRS or the IRS has notified you that one of the years for which you are requesting a transcript involved **identity theft** on your federal tax return . . . . ☐

Caution. Do not sign this form unless all applicable lines have been completed.

Signature of taxpayer(s). I declare that I am either the taxpayer whose name is shown on line 1a or 2a, or a person authorized to obtain the tax information requested. If the request applies to a joint return, at least one spouse must sign. If signed by a corporate officer, partner, guardian, tax matters partner, executor, receiver, administrator, trustee, or party other than the taxpayer, I certify that I have the authority to execute Form 4506-T on behalf of the taxpayer. **Note.** For transcripts being sent to a third party, this form must be received within 120 days of the signature date.

Phone number of taxpayer on line 1a or 2a
(12)

Sign Here
▶ (10) Signature (see instructions) (11) Date
▶ (13) Title (if line 1a above is a corporation, partnership, estate, or trust)
▶ (14) Spouse's signature (15) Date

For Privacy Act and Paperwork Reduction Act Notice, see page 2. Cat. No. 37667N Form **4506-T** (Rev. 9-2013)

The instructions listed below are recommendations for how a loan applicant is to complete a portion of the form. The SBA lender will complete your partially completed form following the formal instruction included on the IRS Form 4506-T. This form can be downloaded from www.ApprovedBook.com.

To complete the 4506-T, only complete the sections that are marked on the sample 4506-T. The SBA lender will complete the other sections on your behalf and request your signature on the completed form at a later date. Some lenders may request that you just sign the bottom of the form so they can complete copies of this form in cases where you have several companies.

1. Name shown on tax return: Enter the business name as it is shown on the business tax return. If the business is reported on the Schedule C of an individual's tax return (IRS Form 1040), enter the taxpayer's name exactly as it appears on the most recently filed individual tax return.

2. First Social Security number or employer identification number: Enter the business's employer identification number (EIN) as listed in the top right corner of the most recent business tax return. If the business is reported on the Schedule C of an individual's tax return (IRS Form 1040), enter the first Social Security number.

3. Spouse's name: If the business is reported on the Schedule C of an individual tax return (IRS Form 1040), enter the spouse's name exactly as it appears on the most recently filed individual tax return. Otherwise, leave this section blank.

4. Second Social Security number: Only enter a number here if the business is reported on the Schedule C of an individual's tax return (IRS Form 1040). Enter the second Social Security number. A Social Security number should only be listed here if a spouse's name was listed to the left of this field on the form.

5. Current address: Enter the business's current address.

6. Previous address: If the address listed on the most recent business tax return is different from the current address, list the address that appears on the most recent business tax return.

7. Transcript mailing information: Leave this section blank.

8. Transcript requested: Leave this section blank.
9. Year or period requested: Leave this section blank.
10. Signature: If an individual is listed for #1, that individual is to sign here. If a business (entity) is listed for #1, an owner (officer or partner with signature authority) of the entity as of the most recently filed tax period is to sign here.
11. (Signature) date: The individual who signed the form (#10) is to date the form as of the date signed in mm/dd/yyyy format.
12. Phone number: Enter the cell phone (or other direct) number for the individual signing the form (#10).
13. Title: Enter the title of the owner signing on behalf of the company.
14. Spouse's signature: If an individual is listed (#3), this spouse is to sign here.
15. (Spouse's signature) date: Enter the date signed in mm/dd/yyyy.

Now that you have finished the IRS Form 4506-T application page, print this off and put it in a three-ring binder with the corresponding company's last three years of business tax returns. Be sure to prepare an IRS Form 4506-T for each of your companies for which you have 20% or greater ownership.

CHAPTER 16

BUSINESS INFORMATION AND HISTORY FORM

The business information and history template is your opportunity to provide the lender with information about the past, present, and future of the company. If the business is at all specialized, as many businesses are, it is important to provide a high-level description of the company and the products and services offered.

The business information and history template pictured on the left has been numbered to correspond with instructions detailed below. If you have a question about how to complete the form correctly, match the number on the picture to the corresponding number below for detailed instructions. This form should be completed by the delegated primary contact person.

From the top of the business information and history form, completion of the form is as follows:

1. <u>Company name</u>: List the legal name of the operating company as was done at the top of the business loan application summary.

Business Information and History

COMPANY NAME: _____ (1) _____

HISTORY OF THE COMPANY: (year founded, by whom, products and services sold, marketing strategy, sales strategy, location, etc.)

(2)

FUTURE PLANS FOR THE COMPANY: (growth strategy, future opportunities, new products/services)

(3)

WHO ARE THE MANAGERS AND KEY EMPLOYEES OF THE COMPANY?

(4)

	Name	Job Title	Responsibilities	Years w/co.	Salary
1					
2					
3					
4					
5					

WHO ARE THE PRIMARY CUSTOMERS?

(5)

	Customer Name	Location	Percentage (%) of Sales	Payment Terms Offered
1				
2				
3				
4				
5				

WHO ARE THE MAJOR SUPPLIERS?

(6)

	Supplier Name	Location	Supplier Percentage (%)	Payment Terms Offered
1				
2				
3				
4				
5				

WHO ARE THE MAJOR COMPETITORS?

(7)

	Competitors Name	Location	Competing Product/Service	Why Applicant Product/Service is Better
1				
2				
3				
4				
5				

WHAT ARE THE COMPANIES COMPETITIVE ADVANTAGES?

(8)

HOW WILL THIS LOAN BENEFIT THE COMPANY?

(9)

IF THIS IS A BUSINESS ACQUISITION, WHY IS SELLER SELLING?

(10)

2. <u>History of the company</u>: Provide a summary of the company's history. This should include the year the company was founded, who founded the company, changes in ownership, products and services sold, marketing strategy, sales strategy, and location information. Use bullets to keep the narrative concise. Consider completing the business plan questionnaire in addition to providing this summary.

3. <u>Future plans for the company</u>: Summarize in bullet form the growth strategy, future opportunities, and any new products or services on the horizon. This could include new distribution channels, new marketing strategies, new employment positions, etc.

4. <u>Managers and key employees</u>: List the managers and key employees critical to the business. In addition to their full name, provide their title, key job responsibilities, length of time with the company, and salary information.

5. <u>Primary customers</u>: List the customers who represent the largest percentage of the company's sales. If no customer represents more than 5% of your sales, list the types of customers in this column. For location, enter the city and state of your primary customers. Enter the average percentage of sales for each customer. Last, enter if the customer receives any special payment terms such as net 30 versus payment due on sale.

6. <u>Major suppliers</u>: List the suppliers that supply the majority of your inventory or raw goods. For location, enter their city and state. Enter the average percentage of your cost of goods sold that are supplied by these suppliers. Last, enter if the supplier offers any repayment terms other than cash on delivery.

7. <u>Major competitors</u>: List the companies that compete for your customers' business. Include local and national competitors as applicable. For each competitor, list the company name, their location by city and state, their competing product or service, and why your product or service is competitive with theirs.

8. <u>Company's competitive advantages</u>: List the reasons why customers choose your company over the competition.

9. <u>How will this loan benefit the company</u>: Summarize the benefits of obtaining the loan request.

10. If the loan request involves a change in ownership (business acquisition), provide details as to why the seller is selling. Otherwise, enter "N/A."

CHAPTER 17

FINANCIAL PROJECTIONS

The financial projections template is used to estimate the income and expenses of your company over a 12-month period. If your business is a start-up, provide two years of projections. For an existing business, it is typical for lenders to request at least one year of projections. Projections will not be required in situations where the requested financing is supported by historical tax returns; however, lenders prefer to collect them because they provide insight into the future success of your company.

The financial projections template pictured has been numbered from #1 to #54 to correspond with instructions detailed below. If you have a question about how to complete the form correctly, match the number on the picture to the corresponding number below for detailed instructions. This form should be completed by the delegated primary contact person.

From the top left of the financial projections worksheet, complete the form as follows:

Financial Projections Company Name: ① ______ Financial Projection Assumptions Must Be Attached.

Month:	1	2	3	4	5	6	7	8	9	10	11	12	FULL YEAR	%
Starting Cash:	②	$0	$0	$0	$0	$0	$0	$0	$0	$0	$0	$0		
REVENUES														
Gross Receipts:	③												㉛ $0	000.00%
Cost of Goods Sold:	④												㉜ $0	000.00%
Gross Profit:	⑤ $0	$0	$0	$0	$0	$0	$0	$0	$0	$0	$0	$0	㉝ $0	000.00%
Other Income:	⑥												㉞ $0	000.00%
Total Income:	⑦ $0	$0	$0	$0	$0	$0	$0	$0	$0	$0	$0	$0	㉟ $0	000.00%
EXPENSES														
Owner Salaries:	⑧												㊱ $0	000.00%
Emp. Wages & Bene:	⑨												㊲ $0	000.00%
Repairs & Maint:	⑩												㊳ $0	000.00%
Rent:	⑪												㊴ $0	000.00%
Taxes & Licenses:	⑫												㊵ $0	000.00%
Interest:	⑬												㊶ $0	000.00%
Depreciation:	⑭												㊷ $0	000.00%
Amortization:	⑮												㊸ $0	000.00%
Advertising:	⑯												㊹ $0	000.00%
Tele. & Utilities:	⑰												㊺ $0	000.00%
Auto & Truck:	⑱												㊻ $0	000.00%
Accounting & Legal:	⑲												㊼ $0	000.00%
Insurance (all):	⑳												㊽ $0	000.00%
Travel & Ent:	㉑												㊾ $0	000.00%
Office & Supplies:	㉒												㊿ $0	000.00%
All Other:	㉓												(51) $0	000.00%
Total Expenses:	㉔ $0	$0	$0	$0	$0	$0	$0	$0	$0	$0	$0	$0	(52) $0	000.00%
Net Income:	㉕ $0	$0	$0	$0	$0	$0	$0	$0	$0	$0	$0	$0	(53) $0	000.00%
Ending Cash:	㉖ $0	$0	$0	$0	$0	$0	$0	$0	$0	$0	$0	$0	(54)	

㉗ ______ Applicant's Name

㉘ ______ Applicant's Signature

㉙ ______ Date

Yearly to Monthly Calculator

Yearly Amt.	Monthly Amt.
㉚	$0

1. <u>Company name</u>: List the legal name of the operating company as was done at the top of the business loan application summary. The projections should only reflect the income and expenses of this particular company.

Revenues

2. <u>Starting Cash</u>: Enter the amount of working capital (cash) that you will have before you generate any revenue or pay for any expenses detailed on these financial projections. For existing companies, this can be the amount of cash that you have on your balance sheet. If you are not sure what amount to list here, leave it blank. A dollar amount is only to be entered in the first column (month one) of the form.

3. <u>Gross receipts</u>: This represents the amount of income that the business will generate from the sale of your products and services. For example, if you are a paint retailer and you sell paint for $10 a can, your revenue would be $10 times the number of paint cans that you sell. To complete the gross receipts row, enter the amount of revenue that you will generate on a monthly basis starting at month one and ending with month 12. To help you generate reasonable numbers, use the "products and services revenue calculator" that can be downloaded from <u>www.ApprovedBook.com</u>. If revenue is seasonal (up and down depending on the month), be sure that this is represented in this row.

4. <u>Cost of goods sold</u>: This represents the costs directly related to the sale of your products and services. For example, if you are a paint retailer and it costs you four dollars to purchase and receive the paint from your supplier, the four dollars represents your cost of goods sold. Cost of goods sold represents the variable expenses directly related to the product or service that you sell. For manufacturers, cost of goods sold may represent the cost of raw materials plus labor used to manufacture a product for sale. To complete the cost of goods sold row, enter the amount that it will cost you to generate the monthly sales amount listed in step three. Start with month one and end with month 12. To help you generate reasonable numbers, use the "products and services revenue calculator" that can be downloaded from <u>www.ApprovedBook.com</u>.

5. <u>Gross Profit</u>: Gross profit is the difference between gross sales and cost of goods sold. This dollar amount will auto-calculate based on the dollar amounts entered in the gross receipts row and cost of goods sold row.

6. <u>Other Income</u>: Most businesses will generate "other income" that is not the business's primary source of revenue. An example of "other income" is the interest that the business earns from the deposits held at the bank. Leave this row blank unless your business will receive more than $1,000/month of other income. Detail the source of other income in your projection assumptions to be attached to the projections. A projection assumption template is available at www.ApprovedBook.com.

7. <u>Total Income</u>: Total income represents your projected gross profit plus other income. This is the total amount of income that will be available to your business to cover expenses.

Expenses

8. <u>Owner salaries</u>: Owner salary is the combined amount that will be paid to the owners applying for the SBA loan. For an existing company where there is no change in ownership, enter one-twelfth of the amount of owner salary reported on the most recent business tax return in each column. Carry the same monthly expense across the form from month one to month 12 so that the total computed for #36 matches the amount listed on the business tax return. If the monthly expense is expected to increase or decrease so that the annual total does not match the most recent business tax return, enter the projected new amount. Provide an explanation for any increase/decrease to the historical amount in the projection assumptions to be attached. For new companies or transactions involving a change in ownership, you can leave the "owner salaries" row blank. As part of the SBA application, each of the owners will complete a personal income and expense worksheet to identify the amount of owner salary that each owner will require from the business. The SBA lender will use the "personal income and expense forms" to calculate the owner salary deduction amount.

9. Employee wages and benefits: Enter one-twelfth of the employee wage expense as reported on the most recent business tax return. Carry the same monthly expense across the form from month one to month 12 so that the total computed for #37 matches the amount listed on the return. If the monthly expense is expected to increase or decrease so that the annual total does not match the most recent business tax return, enter the projected new amount. Provide an explanation for any increase/decrease to the historical amount in the projection assumptions to be attached. For a new company, provide an estimate of these expenses with a narrative describing how this dollar amount was computed.

10. Repairs and maintenance: Enter one-twelfth of the repairs and maintenance expense as reported on the most recent business tax return. Carry the same monthly expense across the form from month one to month 12 so that the total computed for #38 matches the amount listed on the return. If the monthly expense is expected to increase or decrease so that it does not match the most recent business tax return, enter the projected new amount. Provide an explanation for any increase/decrease to the historical amount in the projection assumptions to be attached. For a new company, provide an estimate of these expenses with a narrative describing how this dollar amount was computed.

11. Rent: Enter one-twelfth of the rent expense as reported on the most recent business tax return. Carry the same monthly expense across the form from month one to month 12 so that the total computed for #39 matches the amount listed on the return. If the monthly expense is expected to increase or decrease so that it does not match the most recent return, enter the projected new amount. Provide an explanation for any increase/decrease to the historical amount in the projection assumptions to be attached. For a new company, provide an estimate of the rent expenses with a narrative describing how this dollar amount was computed.

12. Taxes and licenses: Enter one-twelfth of the taxes and licenses expense as reported on the most recent business tax return. Carry the same monthly expense across the form from month one to month 12 so that the total

computed for #40 matches the amount listed on the return. If the monthly expense is expected to increase or decrease so that it does not match the most recent return, enter the projected new amount. Provide an explanation for any increase/decrease to the historical amount in the projection assumptions to be attached. For a new company, provide an estimate for taxes and licenses with a narrative describing how this dollar amount was computed.

13. Interest: Enter one-twelfth of the interest expense as reported on the most recent business tax return. Carry the same monthly expense across the form from month one to month 12 so that the total computed for #41 matches the amount listed on the return. If the monthly expense is expected to increase or decrease so that it does not match the most recent return, enter the projected new amount. If you are unsure how the financing will impact the interest expense, leave this row blank. Provide an explanation for any increase/decrease to the historical amount in the projection assumptions to be attached.

14. Depreciation: Enter one-twelfth of the depreciation expense as reported on the most recent business tax return. Carry the same monthly expense across the form from month one to month 12 so that the total computed for #42 matches the amount listed on the return. If the monthly expense is expected to increase or decrease so that it does not match the most recent return, enter the projected new amount. Provide an explanation for any increase/decrease to the historical amount in the projection assumptions to be attached. For a new company or if you are unsure how to estimate depreciation, leave this row blank.

15. Amortization: Enter one-twelfth of the amortization expense as reported on the most recent business tax return. The amortization expense is usually reported as part of the "other deductions" exhibit on the return. Carry the same monthly expense across the form from month one to month 12 so that the total computed for #43 matches the amount listed on the return. If the monthly expense is expected to increase or decrease so that it does not match the most recent return, enter the projected new amount. Provide an explanation for any increase/decrease to the

historical amount in the projection assumptions to be attached. For a new company or if you are unsure how to estimate amortization, leave this row blank.

16. <u>Advertising</u>: Enter one-twelfth of the advertising expense as reported on the most recent business tax return. Carry the same monthly expense across the form from month one to month 12 so that the total computed for #44 matches the amount listed on the return. If the monthly expense is expected to increase or decrease so that it does not match the most recent return, enter the projected new amount. Provide an explanation for any increase/decrease to the historical amount in the projection assumptions to be attached. For a new company, provide an estimate for advertising with a narrative describing how this dollar amount was computed.

17. <u>Telephone and utilities</u>: Enter one-twelfth of the telephone and utilities expense as reported on the most recent business tax return. Carry the same monthly expense across the form from month one to month 12 so that the total computed for #45 matches the amount listed on the return. If the monthly expense is expected to increase or decrease so that it does not match the most recent business tax return, enter the projected new amount. Provide an explanation for any increase/decrease to the historical amount in the projection assumptions to be attached. For a new company, provide an estimate for telephone and utilities with a narrative describing how this dollar amount was computed.

18. <u>Auto and truck</u>: Enter one-twelfth of the auto and truck expense as reported on the most recent business tax return. Carry the same monthly expense across the form from month one to month 12 so that the total computed for #46 matches the amount listed on the return. If the monthly expense is expected to increase or decrease so that it does not match the most recent return, enter the projected new amount. Provide an explanation for any increase/decrease to the historical amount in the projection assumptions to be attached. For a new company, provide an estimate for auto and truck expenses with a narrative describing how this dollar amount was computed.

19. <u>Accounting and legal</u>: Enter one-twelfth of the accounting and legal expense as reported on the most recent business tax return. Carry the same monthly expense across the form from month one to month 12 so that the total computed for #47 matches the amount listed on the return. If the monthly expense is expected to increase or decrease so that it does not match the most recent tax return, enter the projected new amount. Provide an explanation for any increase/decrease to the historical amount in the projection assumptions to be attached. For a new company, provide an estimate for accounting and legal expenses with a narrative describing how this dollar amount was computed.

20. <u>Insurance (all)</u>: Enter one-twelfth of the insurance expense as reported on the most recent business tax return. Carry the same monthly expense across the form from month one to month 12 so that the total computed for #48 matches the amount listed on the return. If the monthly expense is expected to increase or decrease so that it does not match the most recent return, enter the projected new amount. Provide an explanation for any increase/decrease to the historical amount in the projection assumptions to be attached. For a new company, provide an estimate for insurance expenses with a narrative describing how this dollar amount was computed.

21. <u>Travel and entertainment</u>: Enter one-twelfth of the travel and entertainment expense as reported on the most recent business tax return. Carry the same monthly expense across the form from month one to month 12 so that the total computed for #49 matches the amount listed on the return. If the monthly expense is expected to increase or decrease so that it does not match the most recent return, enter the projected new amount. Provide an explanation for any increase/decrease to the historical amount in the projection assumptions to be attached. For a new company, provide an estimate for travel and entertainment with a narrative describing how this dollar amount was computed.

22. <u>Office and supplies</u>: Enter one-twelfth of the office and supplies expense as reported on the most recent business tax return. Carry the same monthly expense across the form from month one to month 12 so that

the total computed for #50 matches the amount listed on the return. If the monthly expense is expected to increase or decrease so that it does not match the most recent return, enter the projected new amount. Provide an explanation for any increase/decrease to the historical amount in the projection assumptions to be attached. For a new company, provide an estimate for office and supplies expense with a narrative describing how this dollar amount was computed.

23. <u>All other</u>: The "all other" expense represents all of the other expense line items not previously covered. At the bottom of your business tax return, you will have an "other deductions" line item. Take this dollar amount and subtract the items such as amortization, utility expense, and any other expense that was previously accounted for on the form. Enter one-twelfth of the adjusted "other deductions" amount in this section. Carry the same monthly expense across the form from month one to month 12. If the monthly expense is expected to increase or decrease so that it does not match the most recent business tax return, enter the projected new amount. Provide an explanation for any increase/decrease to the historical amount in the projection assumptions to be attached. For a new company, provide an estimate for "all other" with a narrative describing how this dollar amount was computed.

24. <u>Total expenses</u>: Total monthly expenses will be calculated automatically by the form.

25. <u>Net income</u>: Total monthly net income will be calculated automatically by the form.

26. <u>Ending cash</u>: The ending cash figures will calculate automatically, providing you with information about the amount of cash in your business that you expect to have at the end of each month.

27. <u>Applicant's name</u>: The name of the individual loan applicant who completed the financial projections should be listed here.

28. <u>Applicant's signature</u>: The signature of the individual loan applicant who completed the financial projections should be listed here.

29. <u>Date</u>: The date that the financial projections were prepared should be entered here using mm/dd/yyyy format.

30. <u>Monthly calculator</u>: The calculator in the bottom right serves as a tool to quickly complete this form using historical tax returns without needing a calculator.

31. <u>(#31-54) Full year</u>: The totals listed here represent the compiled total for each of the line items on an annual basis. These dollar amounts will be compared to previously filed business tax returns. Any amounts that appear to be irregular from a historical perspective should be addressed in the projection assumptions to be attached to the projections.

Once you have completed your financial projections template, prepare a short narrative to discuss how you generated your numbers. For example, if sales are expected to increase, provide details of the reasons they will increase (for example, that you just signed a large contract or you will be doing a new marketing campaign, etc.). Compare each projected line item total with the dollar amount represented for that line item on the previous tax return. Note whether you are projecting the dollar amount for the line item to be consistent with or to change from the previous year. Provide a simple explanation for any change.

CHAPTER 18

PERSONAL FINANCIAL STATEMENT— SBA FORM 413

The SBA's personal financial statement (SBA Form 413) is a form created, updated, and required by the SBA. The form serves several purposes including assisting lenders (and the SBA) determine SBA loan eligibility (discussed in Part Two) and evaluating your credit profile (discussed in Part Three). The personal financial statement (PFS) is a representation of your personal assets and liabilities. This form can be confusing and questions about how to complete it correctly are common.

The personal financial statement (PFS) is to be completed by each of the business owners specified on the business loan application summary form who have or will have a 20% or greater ownership interest. If no owner has at least a 20% ownership interest, at least one of the owners will be required to guaranty the loan and will be required to complete this form.

The SBA loan programs are federal programs, so the SBA's personal financial statement is a representation of the personal assets and liabilities of the individuals listed at the top of your federal income tax return (IRS

Form 1040). If you file a joint tax return, the PFS should represent assets and liabilities that are held both jointly (with your spouse) and individually. The SBA Form 413 is a great form to summarize your personal assets and liabilities. The first page is a summary of these. The second page is where your summarized assets and liabilities listed on page one are broken down to detail each of your assets and liabilities. The third page is a continuation of the second page in addition to a section for signatures (by both spouses) to certify that the information provided is accurate. If all of your assets and liabilities cannot be itemized on the second and third page, download the PFS Addendum from www.ApprovedBook.com. The PFS Addendum will enable you to list far more assets and liabilities, giving you and the lender a complete understanding of the assets and liabilities of your household.

As a reminder, assets that are owned and liabilities that are paid by third parties such as an LLC are not to be listed on your personal financial statement. If a car loan listed on your credit report is paid by your business, the car should be listed on your business's balance sheet in the asset section and the loan should be listed on the liability section of the balance sheet. The car should not be listed on your personal financial statement. This is important because you obviously do not want liabilities to be doubled by the lender in its analysis of your credit worthiness.

The Personal Financial Statement (pictured) has been numbered to correspond with the written explanation of how to complete each of the fields. If there is a field on the form that causes you confusion, find the corresponding number for detailed instructions. Listed below are the step-by-step instructions on how to complete the SBA Form 413 (Personal Financial Statement). The electronic version of this form has an auto-calculate feature which is available for download at www.ApprovedBook.com.

From the top of page one of the personal financial statement (SBA Form 413), complete the form as follows:

1. <u>As of</u>: List the date that you complete the personal financial statement. The date should be listed in mm/dd/yyyy format.

OMB APPROVAL NO.: 3245-0188
EXPIRATION DATE: 01/31/2018

PERSONAL FINANCIAL STATEMENT
7(a) / 504 LOANS AND SURETY BONDS

U.S. SMALL BUSINESS ADMINISTRATION   As of ____(1)____, _____

SBA uses the information required by this Form 413 as one of a number of data sources in analyzing the repayment ability and creditworthiness of an application for an SBA guaranteed 7(a) or 504 loan or a guaranteed surety.

Complete this form for: (1) each proprietor; (2) general partner; (3) managing member of a limited liability company (LLC); (4) each owner of 20% or more of the equity of the Applicant (including the assets of the owner's spouse and any minor children); and (5) any person providing a guaranty on the loan

Return completed form to:
For 7(a) loans: the lender processing the application for SBA guaranty
For 504 loans: the Certified Development Company (CDC) processing the application for SBA guaranty
For Surety Bonds: the Surety Company or Agent processing the application for surety bond guaranty

Name (2)	Business Phone (3)
Home Address (4)	**Home Phone** (5)
City, State, & Zip Code (6)	

Business Name of Applicant (7)

ASSETS	(Omit Cents)	LIABILITIES	(Omit Cents)
Cash on Hand & in banks............................$ ____ (8)		Accounts Payable.................................$ ____ (19)	
Savings Accounts.......................................$ ____ (9)		Notes Payable to Banks and Others.........$ ____ (20)	
IRA or Other Retirement Account...................$ ____ (10)		(Describe in Section 2)	
(Describe in Section 5)		Installment Account (Auto)......................$ ____ (21)	
Accounts & Notes Receivable.......................$ ____ (11)		Mo. Payments $ ____ (22)	
(Describe in Section 5)		Installment Account (Other).....................$ ____ (23)	
Life Insurance – Cash Surrender Value Only......$ ____ (12)		Mo. Payments $ ____ (24)	
(Describe in Section 8)		Loan(s) Against Life Insurance.................$ ____ (25)	
Stocks and Bonds......................................$ ____ (13)		Mortgages on Real Estate.......................$ ____ (26)	
(Describe in Section 3)		(Describe in Section 4)	
Real Estate..$ ____ (14)		Unpaid Taxes.......................................$ ____ (27)	
(Describe in Section 4)		(Describe in Section 6)	
Automobiles...$ ____ (15)		Other Liabilities....................................$ ____ (28)	
(Describe in Section 5, and include		(Describe in Section 7)	
Year/Make/Model)		Total Liabilities....................................$ ____ (29)	
Other Personal Property ....$ ____ (16)		Net Worth..$ ____ (30)	
(Describe in Section 5)			
Other Assets..$ ____ (17)		**Total** $ ____ (31)	
(Describe in Section 5)		*Must equal total in assets column.	
Total $ ____ (18)			

Section 1. Source of Income.		Contingent Liabilities	
Salary..$ ____ (32)		As Endorser or Co-Maker........................$ ____ (36)	
Net Investment Income................................$ ____ (33)		Legal Claims & Judgments......................$ ____ (37)	
Real Estate Income....................................$ ____ (34)		Provision for Federal Income Tax..............$ ____ (38)	
Other Income (Describe below)*.....................$ ____ (35)		Other Special Debt................................$ ____ (39)	

Description of Other Income in Section 1.

(40)

*Alimony or child support payments should not be disclosed in "Other Income" unless it is desired to have such payments counted toward total income.

2. <u>Name</u>: List your full name (and spouse's full name) as it appears on the top of your personal tax return (IRS Form 1040). If taxes are filed jointly, both names must be reflected here regardless of ownership in the applicant business.

3. <u>Business phone:</u> List the direct work phone number for the person most likely to be contacted regarding the business loan application. A general business phone number can cause delays in communication, particularly related to confidential information.

4. <u>Home address</u>: List the street address where you live. This should not be your business address. It should match the address listed on your driver's license and credit report.

5. <u>Residence phone</u>: List your home number or the cell phone number for the person most likely to be contacted regarding the business loan application.

6. <u>City, state, and zip code</u>: Complete this section to match the street address listed for #4 (residence address).

7. <u>Business name of applicant/borrower</u>: Leave this section blank. It is common for businesses to operate under several names and many times, new entities are created for the purpose of obtaining financing. This will be completed by the lender during the underwriting process.

Assets

The left side of the bottom half of the first page is a summary of your personally held assets.

8. <u>Cash on hand and in banks</u>: List the total amount of cash that you keep liquid for monthly expenses (bills) and general spending money. This should be the total balance of all of your personal checking accounts (individually held and jointly held) plus any cash under your mattress, in the sock drawer, and in your wallet.

9. <u>Saving accounts</u>: Enter the total balance of cash held in your various savings accounts. This should include individual and joint personal savings accounts and certificates of deposit (CDs) held at your bank. This should also include savings in 529 plans and HSA accounts.

10. <u>IRA or other retirement account</u>: Enter the total current balance of all of your 401(k)'s, IRAs, and other retirement accounts. This should include all accounts that would incur a penalty by the government if you were to take an early withdrawal (i.e., prior to age 59 ½). Bankers like to see retirement accounts because even though these accounts are not as liquid as cash or marketable securities, they can be drawn from in an emergency to potentially save a business, and they indicate that the applicant is planning ahead. Additional details regarding the IRA and other retirement accounts are to be detailed in section five on page two of this form.

11. <u>Accounts and notes receivable</u>: Enter the total amount of money due to you by a third party. This could be a loan that you made to your business, to a friend, or a family member. It could also be for work that you did for someone that you will be paid for personally (in your individual name, not your business).

12. <u>Life insurance cash surrender value</u>: Only list a value here if you have a whole life insurance policy. Term life policies do not have a cash surrender value. If you have a whole life policy, your statement should indicate the cash surrender value. The full details of any life insurance policy are to be listed in section eight on page three of this form.

13. <u>Stocks and bonds</u>: List the total value of all of your marketable securities held by you and your spouse. Consider compiling your marketable security information on the PFS Addendum available to be downloaded from www.ApprovedBook.com. Additional details regarding stocks and bonds are to be detailed in section three on page two of this form.

14. <u>Real estate</u>: Enter the total market value of all of your personally held real estate. It should include your primary residence, all other residences, and any other properties (including investment properties) held personally. The value of each of the properties should be based on the current market. It is common for people to list a value much higher than the price that was paid for the residence. Unless you have made substantial improvements to the property, I would recommend not inflating the value unless you can back it up with an appraisal or Internet comps.

Additional details regarding personally held real estate are to be detailed in section four on page two of this form.

15. Automobiles: Enter the total value of all of your personally titled cars as well as boats, RVs, four-wheelers, and other motorized vehicles. If any of these automobiles are represented on a business's balance sheet or paid for by a third party (business), do not list them on the personal financial statement. Provide additional details regarding model year, make, and model in section five on page two of this form.

16. Other personal property: Enter the total value for all other personal assets. Examples of other personal property include jewelry, artwork, antiques, electronics, furniture, and collectibles. Additional details regarding other personal property are to be detailed in section five on page two of this form.

17. Other assets: List the value of your personal ownership interest in private businesses. For example, if you have 25% interest in a business that has a net worth of $1 million, list $250,000 for other assets. The details of your other assets are to be listed in section five on page two of this form.

18. Total: Enter the total value of all of the assets listed for #8 through #17 on this form. This total should represent the total value of all of your personally owned assets.

Liabilities

The right side of the first page (bottom half) is for your personal liabilities and net worth. When completing the right side of this form, print off all of your current loan and credit card statements and download a copy of your free credit reports. To get a copy of your free credit report, go to www.annualcreditreport.com. The SBA lender will obtain a copy of your credit report so it is important that you have a copy and current debt statements to accurately complete the liability portion of your personal financial statement.

19. Accounts payable: Enter the total amount of bills that are unpaid as of the date of this form. An example of an account payable is your cable bill that is outstanding. Accounts payable is typically left blank or zero.

20. Notes payable: Enter the total amount of personal debt that is owed based on a formal agreement. Credit cards and personal lines of credit are the most common type of notes payable. All payables are considered to be short-term liabilities and are expected to be paid within the year. All of your notes payables are to be detailed on page two of this form in section two. Make sure to enter the actual total balance as of the date of this form regardless of whether you pay the entire balance every month.

21. Installment account (auto): Enter the total outstanding balance of all of your car, boat, and plane loans. On your credit report, you will usually see "auto" listed next to any car loans.

22. Monthly payment (auto): Enter the total monthly payment based on the total balance listed for #21.

23. Installment account (other): Enter the total balance of all other term loans (non-auto). Other installment accounts include personal loans, furniture loans, student loans, and other loans that have a scheduled monthly payment and are payable over more than one year.

24. Monthly payment (other): Enter the total monthly payment based on the total balance listed for #23.

25. Loan on life insurance: Enter the outstanding balance of any loan that you have taken against your life insurance policy. This would be an amount that you have borrowed against the cash value listed for #12.

26. Mortgages on real estate: Enter the total balance of all personal mortgage debt (including home equity lines of credit). The amount listed here will be further detailed in section four on page two of this form. If you have more than three mortgages in your personal name, download the PFS Addendum from www.ApprovedBook.com.

27. Unpaid taxes: Taxes include all taxes for which you are personally liable such as income tax and real estate tax. Enter zero unless you owe taxes that are past due. If your taxes are past due provide details of the delinquency including negotiated repayment terms in section six on page two.

28. Other liabilities: Enter the total balance of any other liabilities that you owe that have not been entered in any other section. An example of an

"other liability" is past due child support. Detail these other liabilities in section seven on page two.

29. <u>Total liabilities</u>: Enter the total of all liability balances of # 19 (accounts payable) through # 28 (other liabilities), excluding monthly payment amounts listed for # 22 and #24 on this form. This total liability should represent the total amount of money that you (and your spouse) personally owe third parties.

30. <u>Net worth</u>: Enter the difference between your total assets (#18) and total liabilities (#29). This number can be positive or negative.

31. <u>Total</u>: Enter the number calculated from adding net worth (#30) and total liabilities (#29) together. This number should equal the number listed for #18.

Section 1. Source of Income and Contingent Liabilities

32. <u>Salary</u>: Enter the total gross income that you (and your spouse) collect on an annual basis as of the date of this form.

33. <u>Net investment income</u>: Enter the total amount of income generated from your investments, including dividend income.

34. <u>Real estate income</u>: Enter your net income as reported on Schedule E of your personal tax return (Form 1040 Schedule E).

35. <u>Other income</u>: Enter the amount of annual income that you collect from other sources. An example of other income might be money that you collect as a distribution from a business in which you have an ownership interest.

36. <u>As endorser</u>: Enter the amount of outstanding debt for which you have cosigned. For example, if you have cosigned on your child's car loan, enter the outstanding balance here.

37. <u>Legal claims and judgments</u>: Enter the total amount of legal claims and judgments filed against you. If you are a defendant in a lawsuit, enter the amount of the claim against you.

38. <u>Provision for federal income tax</u>: This is for your estimated income tax payment. Most people leave this blank or zero.

39. <u>Other special debt</u>: This is for any other contingent liabilities. This is usually left blank or zero.

40. <u>Description of other income</u>: Detail the source of the other income represented for #35.

<<Insert Pic 8-2 Personal Financial Statement – Pg2 (full page)>>

Section 2. Notes Payable to Banks and Others

41. <u>Name and address of noteholder(s)</u>: List the creditors' names and account numbers for all of your noteholders. These accounts will be matched to the creditors listed on your credit report. If you have more than five creditors, download the PFS Addendum from <u>www.ApprovedBook.com</u>.

42. <u>Original balance</u>: List the greater credit limit or original balance for each of the creditors listed for #41.

43. <u>Current balance</u>: List the current balance for each of the creditors listed for #41. Verify that the amount listed on your statement matches the amount listed on your credit report. The total of all current balances listed should match the total represented for #20 on page one.

44. <u>Payment amount</u>: List the minimum payment amount required by the creditor.

45. <u>Frequency</u>: Enter how often payments are required to be made. Normally, this will be monthly.

46. <u>How secured</u>: Enter what collateral was taken to secure the note. Most credit cards are unsecured. If the account is unsecured, enter "unsecured."

Section 3. Stocks and Bonds

If you have more than four individual stocks and/or bonds, download the PFS Addendum from <u>www.ApprovedBook.com</u>. Keep your marketable security statements in a three-ring binder so that they can easily be submitted to the lender as required.

47. <u>Number of shares</u>: Enter the amount of shares that you own for each marketable security.

Section 2. Notes Payable to Banks and Others. (Use attachments if necessary. Each attachment must be identified as part of this statement and signed.)

Names and Addresses of Noteholder(s)	Original Balance	Current Balance	Payment Amount	Frequency (monthly, etc.)	How Secured or Endorsed Type of Collateral
(41)	(42)	(43)	(44)	(45)	(46)

Section 3. Stocks and Bonds. (Use attachments if necessary. Each attachment must be identified as part of this statement and signed.)

Number of Shares	Name of Securities	Cost	Market Value Quotation/Exchange	Date of Quotation/Exchange	Total Value
(47)	(48)	(49)	(50)	(51)	(52)

Section 4. Real Estate Owned. (List each parcel separately. Use attachment if necessary. Each attachment must be identified as a part of this statement and signed.)

	Property A	Property B	Property C
Type of Real Estate (e.g. Primary Residence, Other Residence, Rental Property, Land, etc.)	(53)		
Address	(54)		
Date Purchased	(55)		
Original Cost	(56)		
Present Market Value	(57)		
Name & Address of Mortgage Holder	(58)		
Mortgage Account Number	(59)		
Mortgage Balance	(60)		
Amount of Payment per Month/Year	(61)		
Status of Mortgage	(62)		

Section 5. Other Personal Property and Other Assets. (Describe, and, if any is pledged as security, state name and address of lien holder, amount of lien, terms of payment and, if delinquent, describe delinquency.)

(63)

Section 6. Unpaid Taxes. (Describe in detail as to type, to whom payable, when due, amount, and to what property, if any, a tax lien attaches.)

(64)

Section 7. Other Liabilities. (Describe in detail.)

(65)

48. <u>Name of security</u>: Enter the name of the stock, bond, or fund.

49. <u>Cost</u>: Enter the amount originally paid for the marketable security.

50. <u>Market value</u>: Enter the current market value for each security. The combined market value for all securities listed should equal the amount listed for #13 on page one.

51. <u>Date</u>: Enter the date of valuation of the market value.

52. <u>Total value</u>: Enter the total current value for each security.

Section 4. Real Estate Owned

This section is where you can list up to three properties. If you have more than three properties owned in your personal name, download the PFS Addendum from www.ApprovedBook.com. As a reminder, this section is only for real estate that is owned in your individual name(s).

53. <u>Type of real estate</u>: Enter if the property is your primary residence, other residence, rental property, land, etc.

54. <u>Address</u>: List the complete physical address of the property including street address, city, state, and zip code.

55. <u>Date purchased</u>: Enter the date the property was acquired.

56. <u>Original cost</u>: Enter the amount originally paid for the property regardless of the additional investments made in the property since the original purchase.

57. <u>Present market value</u>: Enter the current value of the property. Lenders will typically verify the value entered by searching the address on the Internet at popular websites such as zillow.com. If you are not sure of the current value, enter the address in Google and see what it says. The total value for all of your properties should match the total listed in #14 on page one.

58. <u>Name and address of mortgage holder</u>: Enter the current name of the mortgage lender to which payments are made. This will be matched to mortgage loans listed on your credit report.

59. <u>Mortgage account number</u>: List your entire mortgage account number as listed on your mortgage statement. Keep a copy of a recent mortgage

statement for each of your mortgages in a three-ring binder to be submitted to the SBA lender as required.

60. Mortgage balance: Provide the mortgage balance as it appears on your most recent statement. If you have more than one mortgage such as a first mortgage and a home equity line of credit on a property, include the first mortgage balance. You will have to handwrite the second mortgage information or complete the PFS Addendum. The total of all of the mortgages should match the amount entered for #26 on page one of the PFS.

61. Amount of payment: Enter the amount of payment that is required to be paid on a monthly basis. This should be your first mortgage minimum payment. If you have a second mortgage, you will have to handwrite the second mortgage payment amount or complete the PFS Addendum.

62. Status of mortgage: Enter the word "current" unless you are 30 days or more behind on your payments.

Section 5. Other Personal Property and Other Assets

63. Other personal property: Describe each of the assets for which you provided a value in sections 10, 11, 15, 16, and 17 on the first page of the PFS. This includes your retirement accounts, your accounts and notes receivable, your automobiles, your personal property, such as your electronics and furniture, and other assets, such as ownership in privately held businesses and patents. For automobiles, detail the year, make, model, and current value. For other personal assets, such as electronics, jewelry, furniture, and artwork, provide a value for each category. Asset values should correspond to the values listed on page one in sections 10, 11, 15, 16, and 17. If any of these other personal assets are financed and the liability has not previously been detailed on the PFS form, detail the lien holders, lien amounts, terms, pledged assets, and other relevant loan information. Due to limited space available, this additional information can be included on the PFS Addendum available for download from www.ApprovedBook.com.

Section 6. Unpaid Taxes

64. Unpaid taxes: A written explanation for unpaid taxes should only be provided if an amount greater than zero was entered for #27 on page one of the PFS. If you are behind on your taxes, provide the type of delinquent tax, when the tax was due, the amount due, and any property addresses connected with the lien. In addition, provide information about repayment terms if these have been negotiated with the creditor (for example, the IRS or your state).

Section 7. Other Liabilities

65. Other liabilities: Detail the terms of the liability amount listed for #28 on page one of the PFS. Include the source of the other liabilities, the type of liability, to whom payable, balance due, payment amount, maturity date, and any collateral pledged to secure the liability. Other liabilities should not be confused with contingent liabilities. Other liabilities are debts that are required to be repaid personally.

Section 8. Life Insurance Held

66. Life insurance: List all life insurance policies owned by you and your spouse. Term insurance is life insurance that is only payable if the owner dies during a specific period of time. Term life insurance does not have a cash value. Whole life insurance will have a face value (total amount of the coverage) and a smaller cash value. Provide the owner of the policy, the face amount, the cash surrender value, the name of insurance company, and beneficiaries. The total cash surrender value should match the amount listed for #12.

Certification

67. Signature: Each spouse is to sign one of the signature lines and print their name below (#68).

68. Print name: Clearly print or type the full name of the spouse corresponding with signatures.

69. Date: Enter the date the form was signed.

Section 8. Life Insurance Held. (Give face amount and cash surrender value of policies – name of insurance company and Beneficiaries.)

(66)

I authorize the SBA/Lender/Surety Company to make inquiries as necessary to verify the accuracy of the statements made and to determine my creditworthiness.

CERTIFICATION: (to be completed by each person submitting the information requested on this form)

By signing this form, I certify under penalty of criminal prosecution that all information on this form and any additional supporting information submitted with this form is true and complete to the best of my knowledge. I understand that SBA or its participating Lenders or Certified Development Companies or Surety Companies will rely on this information when making decisions regarding an application for a loan or a surety bond. I further certify that I have read the attached statements required by law and executive order.

Signature _____(67)_____   Date _____(69)_____

Print Name _____(68)_____   Social Security No. _____(70)_____

Signature _____(67)_____   Date _____(69)_____

Print Name _____(68)_____   Social Security No. _____(70)_____

NOTICE TO LOAN AND SURETY BOND APPLICANTS: **CRIMINAL PENALITIES AND ADMINISTRATIVE REMEDIES FOR FALSE STATEMENTS:**

Knowingly making a false statement on this form is a violation of Federal law and could result in criminal prosecution, significant civil penalties, and a denial of your loan or surety bond application. A false statement is punishable under 18 U.S.C. §§ 1001 and 3571 by imprisonment of not more than five years and/or a fine of up to $250,000; under 15 U.S.C. § 645 by imprisonment of not more than two years and/or a fine of not more than $5,000; and, if submitted to a Federally-insured institution, a false statement is punishable under 18 U.S.C. § 1014 by imprisonment of not more than thirty years and/or a fine of not more than $1,000,000. Additionally, false statements can lead to treble damages and civil penalties under the False Claims Act, 31 U.S.C. § 3729 and other administrative remedies including suspension and debarment.

PLEASE NOTE: The estimated average burden hours for the completion of this form is 1.5 hours per response. If you have questions or comments concerning this estimate or any other aspect of this information, please contact Chief, Administrative Branch, U.S. Small Business Administration, Washington, D.C. 20416, and Clearance officer, paper Reduction Project (3245-0188), Office of Management and Budget, Washington, D.C. 20503. PLEASE DO NOT SEND FORMS TO OMB.

70. <u>Social Security number</u>: Enter the Social Security number for the name printed to the left of this field. Use XXX-XX-XXXX format.

Once the SBA's personal financial statement has been completed, save the completed form in a three-ring binder with a copy of all of the financial statements used to compile your financial information. During the loan process, having the supporting information available will help you answer any follow-up questions by the lender about your personal financial statement. In addition, some of these statements may be requested as part of underwriting.

CHAPTER 19

PERSONAL INCOME AND EXPENSE

The SBA recommends using a personal income and expense worksheet as a substitute for ratio calculations typically performed by lenders. As discussed in Part Three, lenders can either estimate (guess) your living expenses based on your credit report or be provided a much more precise figure to determine your minimum required living expenses. The purpose of this form is for you to generate an officer salary that covers your family's minimum living expense requirements. This minimum officer salary amount is for underwriting purposes and what you actually pay yourself as an officer of your company is irrelevant to the SBA. For additional information about this, see the personal capacity section in Part Three.

The personal income and expense worksheet (shown below) has been numbered to correspond with this written explanation of how to complete each of the fields. Detailed instructions for each field are provided. Have a copy of your most recent federal income tax return (IRS Form 1040), recent paystubs, a current bank statement, and current loan statements when completing this form. Complete only the sections that are applicable to your family's circumstances.

Personal Income and Expense Form

To be completed by each holder of 20% or more of applicant company.

Name: ①   Spouse's Name: ②

SOURCES OF INCOME		ANNUAL HISTORIC	ANNUAL PROJECTED
③ Gross Salary (Principal):	③		
④ Gross Salary (Spouse):	④		
⑤ Rental Property Income Received (Gross):	⑤		
⑥ Interest Income (Recurring):	⑥		
⑦ Dividend Income (Recurring):	⑦		
⑧ Other Income (Recurring): _____	⑧		
TOTAL SOURCES OF INCOME:		⑨ $0	⑩ $0

USES OF INCOME (EXPENSES)		MONTHLY EXPENSE	ANNUAL EXPENSE
⑪ Mortgage Expense (P&I) / Rent Expense:	⑪		$0
⑫ Rental Property Mortgage Expense:	⑫		$0
⑬ Rental Property Expenses (less depreciation & interest):	⑬	$0	
⑭ Auto Loans (All):	⑭		$0
⑮ Installment Loans (All):	⑮		$0
⑯ Revolving Lines of Credit / Credit Cards (All):	⑯		$0
⑰ Utilities (Gas, Electric, Water, etc.):	⑰		$0
⑱ Phone, Cable & Internet:	⑱		$0
⑲ Income Taxes (Historical Rate):	⑲	$0	
⑳ Property Taxes (Historical Rate):	⑳	$0	
㉑ Alimony and Child Support (if applicable):	㉑		$0
㉒ Tuition Payments:	㉒		$0
㉓ Medical Expenses:	㉓		$0
㉔ Insurance Payments (real estate, car, health, etc.):	㉔		$0
㉕ Food (household):	㉕		$0
㉖ Clothing (household):	㉖		$0
㉗ Other Expenses:	㉗		$0
㉘ **TOTAL USES OF INCOME (EXPENSES):**		㉘ $0	
CASH FLOW SURPLUS (DEFICIT):		㉙ $0	㉚ $0

Signature: ㉛   Date: ㉜

The personal income and expense worksheet is to be completed by each of the business owners that will have a 20% or greater ownership interest. Duplicates of this form will need to be provided to and completed by each 20% or greater owner and to all loan guarantors.

From the top of the personal income and expense worksheet, complete the form as follows:

1. Name: List your full name as it appears on the top of your federal income tax return (IRS Form 1040).

2. Spouse's name: List your spouse's full name as it appears on the top of your federal income tax return (IRS Form 1040).

Sources of Income

3. Gross salary (principal): This is the total amount of salary that can be supported by W-2 statements, 1099 statements, and/or paystubs. Enter your gross annual salary received historically under the "annual historic" column. If this income will continue after obtaining the SBA loan, enter the same annual amount in the "annual projected" column. If you are not going to keep the W-2 or 1999 position after obtaining the SBA loan, leave the "annual projected" column blank or enter zero for gross salary (principal).

4. Gross salary (spouse): This is the total amount of salary received by your spouse that can be supported by W-2 statements, 1099 statements, and/or paystubs. Enter your spouse's gross annual salary received historically under the "annual historic" column. If your spouse is going to keep this W-2 or 1099 position after obtaining the SBA loan, enter the same annual amount in the "annual projected" column. If your spouse is not going to keep the W-2 or 1999 position after obtaining the SBA loan, leave the "annual projected" column blank or enter zero for gross salary (spouse).

5. Rental property income received (gross): This is for rental property income reported on Schedule E of your personal tax return. If you reported rental income on your Schedule E, enter the gross income

represented on your last tax return in the "annual historic" column. If you will continue to have rental property income after the SBA loan, enter the gross income in the "annual projected" column. Your gross income should include all money collected from tenants, including pet fees and reimbursed expenses. Preparing a rent roll can be useful to calculate gross income. A sample rent roll is available at www.ApprovedBook.com.

6. Interest income (recurring): This will be listed on Schedule B of your federal income tax return (IRS Form 1040). If you have recurring interest income, enter the amount in the "annual historic" and "annual projected" columns.

7. Dividend income (recurring): This is also listed on Schedule B next to #9 on your federal income tax return (IRS Form 1040). If you have recurring dividend income, enter the amount in the "annual historic" and "annual projected" columns.

8. Other income (recurring): This is for distribution income that you receive from small businesses not affiliated with your loan request. If you receive other income through a distribution, enter the business name in the space provided. In addition, enter the amount earned in the last tax year for "annual historic" and the same amount for "annual projected."

9. Total sources of income (annual historic): This should represent your total income on a historic basis for you and your spouse. This dollar amount should be easy to verify referencing your most recent personal tax return.

10. Total sources of income (annual projected): This should represent your total historic income minus any sources of income that will not continue following the business loan approval and closing.

Uses of Income

To complete the uses of income section, enter dollar amounts that represent your lifestyle at a boring minimum. This is the amount necessary to pay the minimum of your ongoing bills, put food on your table, and cover transportation expenses to and from work. This is a "needs calculation," not a "want calculation." If you have extra money and want to spend $50,000 on vacations and eat out three times a day from personal resources, that is great but don't put that on this form.

To complete this section of the form, have a copy of your most recent personal tax return (IRS Form 1040 with all schedules) and access to your current financial records including bank statements, debt statements, and paystubs.

11. Mortgage expense: This is your total monthly mortgage expense for your primary residence (and personally held properties only used for personal use). On your mortgage statement, your mortgage payment is likely to include a breakdown for principal, interest, real estate taxes, and homeowners insurance expenses. For monthly expense, only enter the total amount paid for your monthly principal and interest expense. Your real estate taxes and insurance will be entered for #20 and #24 below. If you have multiple mortgages on your primary (and secondary) residence, list the total monthly principal and interest (P&I) expense.

12. Rental property mortgage expense: This is only to be completed if you own rental property that is reported on Schedule E of your most recent IRS Form 1040 and you have mortgages on the properties. For all rental properties with mortgages, list the total monthly mortgage payment amount (principal and interest only) for all properties in the monthly column.

13. Rental property expenses: This is only to be completed if you have rental properties that are reported on Schedule E of your most recent personal tax return (IRS Form 1040). On your Schedule E, #20 is total expenses. Take this number and subtract mortgage interest (#12) and depreciation (#18) from it. Enter the calculated amount in the annual expense column.

14. Auto loans: This is for all car payments that you (and your spouse) pay for personally. This includes auto loan monthly payments and auto lease monthly payments. If your business pays your auto loan and lease payments, do not list these payments on the personal income and expense form. If you personally pay auto loans, enter the monthly amount in the monthly expense column.

15. Installment Loans: This is for all nonauto loans such as personal loans (e.g., computer or furniture loans) and student loans. Enter the total monthly amount in the monthly expense column.

16. Revolving lines of credit/credit cards: This is the minimum monthly payment required for all of your credit cards and personal lines of credit. If you have one credit card with debt, enter the minimum payment amount listed on your most recent credit card statement in the monthly expense column. If you are not sure of the minimum payment required, multiply your balance by 3% to estimate your minimum payment. If you have several credit cards, add your minimum credit card payments together and enter the total minimum payment amount in the monthly expense column.

17. Utilities: This represents your monthly utility expense for your primary residence, including gas, electric, water, and trash. Calculate an average monthly expense for utilities and enter this amount in the monthly expense column.

18. Phone, cable, and Internet: This represents your monthly expense for communication, including personal cell phones. The monthly expense typically ranges between $50 and $300. Any expenses paid for by third parties such as your business should not be included.

19. Income tax: This is your household's total for federal and state taxes. To find this number, look at your most recent tax return. Your total federal tax will be listed on page two of your IRS Form 1040 (#61 for the 2013 IRS Form 1040). Your total state tax will be listed next to state and local on Schedule A of your personal tax return (IRS Form 1040 Schedule A #5). Add the federal tax amount to the state tax amount and enter the total in the annual expense column.

20. Property taxes: These are the real estate taxes paid on your primary residence. This amount is listed on Schedule A of your IRS Form 1040. Enter the amount listed next to real estate taxes (#6 for the 2013 IRS Form 1040 Schedule A) in the annual expense column.

21. <u>Alimony and child support</u>: This is only to be completed if you pay alimony and/or child support. Enter the amount paid monthly in the monthly expense column.

22. <u>Tuition payment</u>: This is only to be completed if you make payments toward tuition in addition to payments for student loans covered by installment loans (see #15). This is typically left blank if college tuition will be funded from a college savings account such as a 529 plan.

23. <u>Medical expense</u>: This is your out-of-pocket expense paid for doctor visits, over-the- counter medication, prescription medication, etc. Enter this monthly amount in the monthly expense column. Your medical insurance is covered for #24.

24. <u>Insurance payments</u>: This represents your monthly expense paid for all of your various insurance policies such as health insurance, life insurance, car insurance, and homeowners insurance. Life insurance and health insurance payments are commonly deducted directly from your paycheck. Other insurance payments such as homeowners insurance and car insurance payments can be found on your mortgage statement and bank statements.

25. <u>Food</u>: This represents your monthly food and beverage expense. This includes restaurant and grocery expenses. One thousand dollars is typical for a monthly food budget.

26. <u>Clothing</u>: This represents all household purchases for clothing. If you purchase approximately $2,000 on clothing a year, enter $167/month ($2,000/12 months = $167 per month). If business attire is expensed through your business, your personal clothing expense could be minimal. Fifty dollars is a typical monthly minimum.

27. <u>Other expenses</u>: This includes gas for your car, daycare, and miscellaneous expenses. This is typically between $500 and $2,000 per month.

28. <u>Total uses of income (expense)</u>: This should represent your annual expenses on a mandatory expense level. Money allocated toward investments or vacations should not be reflected in the total. If you can trim your expense budget, do so.

29. <u>Cash flow (annual historic)</u>: This should reflect a positive number. It should reflect that based on your current financial situation, your current income is greater than your expenses.

30. <u>Cash flow (annual projected)</u>: This may be a positive or negative number. If an existing income source will be going away as a result of your business loan request, this projected cash flow number may be a deficit. As discussed in Part Three, the amount listed as a deficit represents the amount necessary for underwriting purposes to be withdrawn from the applicant business as your officer salary. A minimal officer salary is a good thing from a lender's perspective. Remember that your officer salary is a business expense and limiting business expenses increases profitability and your ability to repay business debt.

31. <u>Signature</u>: This line should be signed by the person whose name was entered next to #1.

32. <u>Date</u>: Enter the date that the form was completed and signed.

CHAPTER 20

STATEMENT OF PERSONAL HISTORY– SBA FORM 912

The Statement of Personal History is a form created, maintained, and required by the SBA. The form serves several purposes, including assisting lenders (and the SBA) determine SBA loan eligibility (as discussed in Part Two) and character (as discussed in Part Three). This form can be confusing to complete and approximately 20% or more of the form should be left blank for the SBA lender to finish.

The Statement of Personal History is to be completed by each of the business owners specified on the business loan application summary form who will have 20% or greater ownership interests. The Statement of Personal History is also to be completed by any key managers and employees of the company whose involvement is critical to the success of the business. A separate Statement of Personal History should be completed for each identified individual. Spousal owners who are either critical to the success of the business or have at least a 20% interest in the applicant business are to each complete their own Statement of Personal History. Each owner of at least a 20% ownership interest in the applicant business should be provided with a copy of this form to complete.

The Statement of Personal History (pictured) has been numbered to correspond with a written explanation of how to complete each of the fields. If there is a field that you don't know how to finish, find the corresponding number below for detailed instructions. Listed below are the step-by-step instructions on how to complete the SBA Form 912, also known as the Statement of Personal History. This form is available for download at www.ApprovedBook.com.

The Statement of Personal History is to be completed as follows:

1. Name and address of applicant: **Leave this section blank**. This will be completed by the SBA lender.
2. SBA district office: **Leave this section blank**. This will be completed by the SBA lender.
3. Amount applied for: **Leave this section blank**. This will be completed by the SBA lender.
4. File number: **Leave this section blank**. This will be completed by the SBA lender.
5. Personal statement of (line #1): List the entire first name, entire middle name, and entire last name. If you do not have a middle name, list "NMN." If you only have an initial as your middle name, list your initial. There is space to enter up to three versions of your name, including your full name as it is presently listed on your driver's license and former names such as prior to marriage. Make sure to include alternate names such as your maiden name.
6. Percentage of ownership (line #2): Enter the amount of ownership to be owned upon funding of the SBA loan.
7. Social Security number: Enter your complete Social Security number in XXX-XX-XXXX format.
8. Date of birth (line #3): Enter your date of birth in mm/dd/yyyy format.
9. Place of birth (line #4): Enter the city and state if you were born in the USA. If you were born outside of the USA, enter at least the country of birth.

OMB APPROVAL NO.3245-0178
Expiration Date:

United States of America

SMALL BUSINESS ADMINISTRATION

STATEMENT OF PERSONAL HISTORY

Please Read Carefully: SBA uses Form 912 as one part of its assessment of program eligibility. Please reference SBA Regulations and Standard Operating Procedures if you have any questions about who must submit this form and where to submit it. For further information, please call SBA's Answer Desk at 1-800-U-ASK-SBA (1-800-827-5722), or check SBA's website at www.sba.gov. **DO NOT SEND COMPLETED FORMS TO OMB as this will delay the processing of your application; send forms to the address provided by your lender or SBA representative.**

Name and Address of Applicant (Firm Name)(Street, City, State, and ZIP Code)

①

SBA District/Disaster Area Office

②

Amount Applied for (when applicable)   File No. (if known)

③   ④

1. Personal Statement of: (State name in full, if no middle name, state (NMN), or if initial only, indicate initial.) List all former names used, and dates each name was used. Use separate sheet if necessary.

2. Give the percentage of ownership or stock owned or to be owned in the small business or the development company   Social Security No.

⑥   ⑦

First   Middle   Last

⑤

3. Date of Birth (Month, day, and year)

⑧

4. Place of Birth: (City & State or Foreign Country)

⑨

Name and Address of participating lender or surety co. (when applicable and known)

⑩

5. U.S. Citizen?   YES   NO   ⑪ INITIALS: _____
If No, are you a Lawful   YES   NO
Permanent resident alien:
If non- U.S. citizen provide alien registration number:

6. Present residence address:
From: ⑫
To: ⑬
Address: ⑭

Most recent prior address (omit if over 10 years ago):
From: ⑮
To: ⑯
Address: ⑰

Home Telephone No. (Include Area Code):
Business Telephone No. (Include Area Code): ⑱

PLEASE SEE REVERSE SIDE FOR EXPLANATION REGARDING DISCLOSURE OF INFORMATION AND THE USES OF SUCH INFORMATION.

YOU MUST INITIAL YOUR RESPONSES TO QUESTIONS 5,7,8 AND 9.

IF YOU ANSWER "YES" TO 7, 8, OR 9, FURNISH DETAILS ON A SEPARATE SHEET. INCLUDE DATES, LOCATION, FINES, SENTENCES, WHETHER MISDEMEANOR OR FELONY, DATES OF PAROLE/PROBATION, UNPAID FINES OR PENALTIES, NAME(S) UNDER WHICH CHARGED, AND ANY OTHER PERTINENT INFORMATION. AN ARREST OR CONVICTION RECORD WILL NOT NECESSARILY DISQUALIFY YOU; HOWEVER, AN UNTRUTHFUL ANSWER WILL CAUSE YOUR APPLICATION TO BE DENIED AND SUBJECT YOU TO OTHER PENALTIES AS NOTED BELOW.

7. Are you presently subject to an indictment, criminal information, arraignment, or other means by which formal criminal charges are brought in any jurisdiction?

Yes   No   ⑲   INITIALS: _____

8. Have you been arrested in the past six months for any criminal offense?

Yes   No   ⑳   INITIALS: _____

9. For any criminal offense – other than a minor vehicle violation – have you ever: 1) been convicted; 2) plead guilty; 3) plead nolo contendere; 4) been placed on pretrial diversion; or 5) been placed on any form of parole or probation (including probation before judgment).
Yes   No   ㉑   INITIALS: _____

10. I authorize the Small Business Administration Office of Inspector General to request criminal record information about me from criminal justice agencies for the purpose of determining my eligibility for programs authorized by the Small Business Act, and the Small Business Investment Act.

CAUTION - PENALTIES FOR FALSE STATEMENTS: Knowingly making a false statement on this form is a violation of Federal law and could result in criminal prosecution, significant civil penalties, and a denial of your loan, surety bond, or other program participation. A false statement is punishable under 18 USC 1001 and 3571 by imprisonment of not more than five years and/or a fine of up to $250,000; under 15 USC 645 by imprisonment of not more than two years and/or a fine of not more than $5,000; and, if submitted to a Federally insured institution, under 18 USC 1014 by imprisonment of not more than thirty years and/or a fine of not more than $1,000,000.

Signature   Title   Date
            ㉒   ㉓   ㉔

Agency Use Only   ㉕

11.   Fingerprints Waived   12.   Cleared for Processing   Date   Approving Authority
                        Date   Approving Authority   13.   Request a Character Evaluation
        Fingerprints Required
                        Date   Approving Authority   Date   Approving Authority
Date Sent to OIG   (Required whenever 7, 8 or 9 are answered "yes" even if cleared for processing.)

PLEASE NOTE: The estimated burden for completing this form is 15 minutes per response. You are not required to respond to any collection of information unless it displays a currently valid OMB approval number. If you wish to submit comments on the burden for completing this form, direct these comments to U.S. Small Business Administration, Chief, AIB, 409 3rd St., S.W., Washington D.C. 20416 and Desk Officer for the Small Business Administration, Office of Management and Budget, New Executive Office Building, Room 10202, Washington, D.C. 20503. OMB Approval 3245-0178 DO NOT SEND COMPLETED FORMS TO OMB as this will delay the processing of your application; send forms to the address provided by your lender or SBA representative.

SBA 912 (2-2013) SOP 5010.4 Previous Edition Obsolete

10. <u>Name and address of the participating lender</u>: **Leave this section blank**. This will be completed by the SBA lender.

11. <u>US citizen</u> (line #5): Check "yes" if you are a US citizen and initial your answer. If you are not a US citizen, check "no" and answer if you are a lawful permanent resident alien. If you are not a US citizen but you are a lawful permanent resident alien, check "yes" to the second question and enter your alien registration number. A copy of your permanent resident alien card will be required with submission of this form (as applicable). Make sure to initial next to "initials."

12. <u>From—Present residence address</u> (left side of line #6): Enter the date that you moved to your present home address. The date should be listed in mm/dd/yyyy format. For "dd," list 01 unless you know the exact day.

13. <u>To—Present residence address</u> (left side of line #6): Enter the word "present."

14. <u>Address—Present residence address</u> (left side of line #6): Provide your complete physical street address including city, state, and zip of where you currently live. This is typically your primary residence. Do not list a PO Box.

15. <u>From—Recent prior address</u> (right side of line #6): Enter the date that you moved to your former home address. The date should be listed in mm/dd/yyyy format. For "dd," list 01 unless you know the exact day. If you have lived at your present residence for more than 10 years, you can leave this blank.

16. <u>To—Recent prior address</u> (right side of line #6): Enter the date that you moved to your present residence (to match #12). The date should be listed in mm/dd/yyyy format. If you have lived at your present residence for more than 10 years, you can leave this blank.

17. <u>Address—Recent prior address</u> (right side of line #6): Provide your complete physical street address including the city, state, and zip of where you currently live. This is typically your primary residence. Do not list a PO Box.

18. <u>Home telephone number</u>: Enter either your home number or direct cell phone number. For <u>business telephone number</u>, enter your direct

phone number at your office. Both telephone numbers should be listed in XXX-XXX-XXXX format and will be used by the SBA lender to get in touch with you about your application.

19. <u>Line #7</u>: Answer the question by checking either "yes" or "no" and initialing next to your answer. If you check "yes" to #7, provide details on a separate sheet of paper identifying dates, location, fines, sentences, whether misdemeanor or felony, dates of parole/probation, unpaid fines or penalties, name(s) under which you were charged, and any other pertinent information. A sample 912 exhibit template is available for download from <u>www.ApprovedBook.com</u>.

20. <u>Line #8</u>: Answer the question by checking either "yes" or "no" and initialing next to your answer. If you check "yes" to #8, provide details on a separate sheet of paper identifying dates, location, fines, sentences, whether misdemeanor or felony, dates of parole/probation, unpaid fines or penalties, name(s) under which you were charged, and any other pertinent information. A sample 912 exhibit template is available for download from <u>www.ApprovedBook.com</u>.

21. <u>Line #9</u>: Answer the question by checking either "yes" or "no" and initialing next to your answer. If you check "yes" to #9, provide details on a separate sheet of paper identifying dates, location, fines, sentences, whether misdemeanor or felony, dates of parole/probation, unpaid fines or penalties, name(s) under which you were charged, and any other pertinent information. A sample 912 exhibit template is available for download from <u>www.ApprovedBook.com</u>.

22. <u>Signature</u>: Sign the form. Your signature authorizes the SBA to investigate your answers and determine eligibility for the various SBA programs.

23. <u>Title</u>: Enter "owner" or "manager" or leave it blank.

24. <u>Date</u>: Enter the date signed. Date should be entered in mm/dd/yyyy format.

25. <u>Agency Use Only</u>: Do not write anything in this section.

CHAPTER 21

MANAGEMENT RÉSUMÉ WITH ELIGIBILITY

As discussed in Part Three, the résumé is one of the most important documents that the lender considers in evaluating character. The application résumé is your opportunity to highlight all of your transferable management experience relevant to the applicant business. The SBA lender and the SBA will use this information to evaluate your ability to manage the applicant business. You are in effect applying for the CEO position of the applicant company. Complete the résumé based on your experience as it relates to the roles that you will perform when managing the applicant business.

A management résumé is to be completed by each of the business owners specified on the business loan application summary form who will have 20% or greater ownership interests. A résumé is also to be completed by employees whose involvement is critical to the success of the business. Spousal owners who are either critical to the success of the business or have at least a 20% interest in the applicant business are to complete their own résumé.

The résumé application page (pictured) has been numbered to correspond with the written explanation of how to complete each of the fields. This form can be downloaded from www.ApprovedBook.com.

Management Resume

MANAGER/OWNER INFORMATION *(To be completed by each holder of 20% or more of company ownership, and key management.)*

PERSONAL INFORMATION

First Name: (1)   Middle Name: (2)   Last Name: (3)

Date of Birth: (4)   Place of Birth: (5)   Social Security #: (6)

Phone #'s (H): (7)   (W): (8)   (M): (9)   Email: (10)

Residence Address

Current Address: (11)   City: (12)   State: (13) Zip: (14)

From: (15)   To: Present

Previous Address: (16)   City: (17)   State: (18) Zip: (19)

From: (20)   To: (21)

WORK EXPERIENCE

Company Name: (22)   Location: (23)

From: (24)   To: (25)   Position/Title: (26)

Responsibilities: (27)

Company Name: Location:

From: To: Position/Title:

Responsibilities:

Company Name: Location:

From: To: Position/Title:

Responsibilities:

Company Name: Location:

From: To: Position/Title:

Responsibilities:

EDUCATION

High School/College/Technical-Name	Location	Dates Attended	Degree/Certificate
(28)	(29)	(30) To:	(31)
		To:	
		To:	

MILITARY SERVICE BACKGROUND

Branch of Service: (32)   Dates of Service: (33)   To: Honorable Discharge? ◯ Yes ◯ No (34)

MANAGEMENT QUESTIONS

(35) Are you employed by the U.S. Government? ◯ Yes ◯ No   Agency / Position: _____ (35)

(36) Are you a U.S. Citizen?   ◯ Yes ◯ No   If no, provide Alien Registration Number: _____ (36)

(37) Are you or any of your businesses involved in any lawsuit at this time? ◯ Yes ◯ No   _____ (37)

(38) Have you ever filed for personal or business Bankruptcy protection?   ◯ Yes ◯ No   _____ (38)

(39) Have you been disbarred from doing business with the U.S. Government? ◯ Yes ◯ No   _____ (39)

(40) Do you or your business engage in internet gambling?   ◯ Yes ◯ No   _____ (40)

(41) Have you ever obtained credit under any other name(s)? (list names) ◯ Yes ◯ No   _____ (41)

(42) Are all of your business and personal taxes current?   ◯ Yes ◯ No   _____ (42)

(43) If you have or have ever had any government backed loans, are they presently delinquent? ◯ Yes ◯ No (43)

From the top of the management résumé page, complete the form as follows:

Personal Information

1. <u>First name</u>: Enter your first name as it is listed on your government-issued identification card, such as your driver's license.

2. <u>Middle name</u>: Enter your full middle name as it is listed on your government-issued identification card, such as your driver's license.

3. <u>Last name</u>: Enter your last name as it is listed on your government-issued identification card, such as your driver's license. If you have identifying marks after your last name such as "Jr.," enter this to the right of your last name.

4. <u>Date of birth</u>: Enter your date of birth in mm/dd/yyyy format.

5. <u>Place of birth</u>: Enter your place of birth with city and state if you were born in the USA. If you were born outside of the USA, enter at least the name of the country.

6. <u>Social Security number</u>: Enter your Social Security number in XXX-XX-XXXX format.

7. <u>Home (H) phone number</u>: Enter your home phone number in XXX-XXX-XXXX format. If you do not have a home number, leave this blank.

8. <u>Work (W) phone number</u>: Enter your work phone number in XXX-XXX-XXXX format. This should be your direct phone number at your office. Your lender will be calling this number to discuss confidential business and personal information. It can be uncomfortable for the lender if a receptionist inquires about the purpose of the call.

9. <u>Mobile/cell (M) phone number</u>: Enter your mobile number in XXX-XXX-XXXX format. It is critical for your lender to have direct access to you for application questions and to avoid delays in the process.

10. <u>Email</u>: Enter your personal (nonpublic) email address. The majority of all communication between you and your lender will occur over email. Much of the information communicated will be personal and confidential. Be sure to list an email that you will check regularly and that is private.

11. <u>Current address</u>: Enter the physical address of your primary residence. Do not list a PO Box.

12. <u>City</u>: Enter the city name to match the address listed for #11.

13. <u>State</u>: Enter the state to match the address listed for #11.

14. <u>Zip</u>: Enter the zip code to match the address listed for #11.

15. <u>From</u>: Enter the date that you moved to the address listed in #11. It should be in mm/dd/yyyy format. For "dd," list 01 unless you know the exact day.

16. <u>Previous address</u>: Enter the physical address where you lived just prior to your present address. Do not list a PO Box.

17. <u>City</u>: Enter the city to match the address listed for #16.

18. <u>State</u>: Enter the state to match the address listed for #16.

19. <u>Zip</u>: Enter the zip code to match the address listed for #16.

20. <u>From</u>: Enter the date for when you moved to the address listed in #16. It should be in mm/dd/yyyy format. For "dd," list 01 unless you know the exact day.

21. <u>To</u>: Enter the same date that you entered for #15. It should be in mm/dd/yyyy format.

Work Experience

The management résumé template provides space for up to four companies.

22. <u>Company name:</u> For the first company name, enter your current place of employment. If you work for more than one company, start with the company where your position and responsibilities are most relevant to the business loan application. Enter up to four employers (companies).

23. <u>Location</u>: Enter the city and state or country (if it is/was outside of the USA).

24. <u>From</u>: Enter the date when you started working at the company regardless of your position. Use mm/dd/yyyy formatting and list 01 for "dd" if unknown.

25. <u>To</u>: Enter the date that you left the company. Overlaps in dates are fine. Use mm/dd/yyyy format and list 30 for "dd" if unknown. The top "to" is likely to be "present."

26. Position/title: Enter the highest position that you obtained before leaving the company. If you are/were an owner, enter "owner" and your percent of ownership. If your official title is highly technical or not widely understood, list a more generic title that represents your position such as "operations manager" or "sales manager."

27. Responsibilities: Summarize the responsibilities related to your position listed for #26. Highlight the management aspects versus the technical aspects of the position. This information will be compared to the management requirements of the applicant business. Your responsibilities will be further detailed on page two.

Education

28. High school/college: List the highest level of education that you have obtained. On the next two lines, list organizations where you have obtained certifications relevant to your profession.

29. Location: List the city and state (or country if outside of the USA).

30. Dates attended: List the dates that you started and finished your education in mm/dd/yyyy format.

31. Degree/certificate: Enter the credential acronym and/or the specialty or major such as management. Diploma is fine for high school.

Military

32. If you served in the military, thank you for your service. Enter the branch of service.

33. Dates of service: Enter the year that your service began and the year that you were discharged (yyyy).

34. Honorable discharge: Check "yes" if you received an honorable discharge. Additional loan programs may be available to you.

Management Questions

35. If you are employed by the US government, check "yes" and detail your agency and position.

36. If you are a US citizen, check "yes". If no, check "no" and enter your alien registration number. SBA loans are only eligible for companies that are at least 51% owned by US citizens and lawful permanent residents.

37. If you or any of your businesses are presently involved in a lawsuit (even a minor car accident), check "yes" and briefly describe the source of the lawsuit. In addition to a "yes" response, attach a written explanation describing the circumstances of the lawsuit and how you and the business will be impacted.

38. If you have ever filed for personal or business bankruptcy protection, check "yes" and detail if it was Chapter 7, 11, or 13 and the year. In addition to a "yes" response, attach a written explanation detailing the circumstances that led to the bankruptcy and why another bankruptcy is unlikely in the future.

39. If you are currently disbarred from doing business with the US government, check "yes" and provide an explanation. The present list of disbarred individuals is very short, so you should be well aware of this situation if you are on it.

40. If you engage in paid Internet gambling, check "yes" and enter how often. Free Internet gambling sites for fun do not count. See personal character in Part Three for additional information.

41. If you have ever obtained credit under any other name, check "yes" and detail the other names. This could be maiden names or abbreviations of your name.

42. If you are delinquent on your business or personal taxes, check "yes." If you have not paid your taxes but are still in the grace period, check "no." If yes, attach negotiated IRS or state repayment agreements (if possible).

43. If you have ever had a government loan such as a government-backed student loan, FHA loan, VA loan, or SBA loan and you are presently behind on the loan, check "yes." If you have ever defaulted on a government loan or federal-assisted financing resulting in a loss to the government, check "yes." If yes, attach a written explanation of the default.

Management Resume

MANAGER/OWNER INFORMATION Cont.

APPLICANT BUSINESS SPECIFIC INFORMATION

First Name: (44)　　　　Last Name: (45)

TECHNICAL/BUSINESS EXPERIENCE (relevant to applicant business):

(46)

MANAGEMENT/SUPERVISORY EXPERIENCE (relevant to applicant business):

(47)

EDUCATION/TRAINING (relevant to applicant business):

(48)

ACHIEVEMENTS (relevant to applicant business):

(49)

OTHER ACTIVITIES (Business Associations, Civic Involvement, etc. relevant to applicant business):

(50)

_____ (51)　　　　_____ (52)

Signature　　　　　　　　　Date

Page two of the résumé is for you to detail your transferable experience as it relates to the applicant business. If you will be acquiring a third party's business with SBA loan proceeds, you should obtain a thorough understanding of the current owner's responsibilities. Your ability to perform these responsibilities is to be detailed in this section.

Applicant Business Specific Information

44. First Name: If you are completing this résumé form on your computer, the first name should prefill. Otherwise, enter your first name as it is listed on your government-issued identification card, such as your driver's license.

45. Last Name: If you are completing this résumé form on your computer, the last name should prefill. Otherwise, enter your last name as it is listed on your government-issued identification card, such as your driver's license.

46. Technical/business experience: Describe how your practical experience meets the technical requirements of the applicant business.

47. Management/supervisory experience: Describe how your practical experience meets the supervisory requirements of the applicant business.

48. Education/training: Describe how your education and training has prepared you for management responsibilities of the applicant business.

49. Achievements: Describe any of your accomplishments throughout your career that highlight your ability to set and reach goals.

50. Other activities: List any organizations in which you are active and that are relevant to the applicant business.

51. Signature: Sign the bottom of the résumé.

52. Date: Date the bottom of the résumé in mm/dd/yyyy format.

After you have completed your management résumé, read it over and make sure that you have provided adequate information to justify your business expertise relevant to your responsibilities as an owner of the applicant business.

Attaching additional information about your qualifications to manage your business in bullet form may benefit you and streamline the approval process.

CHAPTER 22

CREDIT AUTHORIZATION

Application—Credit and Background Check Authorization

This form permits the SBA lender and their designated parties to make credit inquiries into everyone that signs this form. Credit reports will be pulled from up to all three credit reporting agencies and additional background checks may be made. SBA lenders require all individuals with 20% or greater ownership to complete and sign a credit authorization form.

1. Name: Enter your first name, middle name, and last name as it is listed on your government-issued driver's license.
2. Signature: Sign the form as you did on your government-issued driver's license.
3. Date: Date the form as of the date the form was signed (mm/dd/yyyy format).
4. Address: Enter your current home address as it is listed on your government-issued driver's license.

Credit Authorization

AUTHORIZATION TO RELEASE INFORMATION

I/We hereby authorize the release to "lender" (**Lender**), of any and all information that **Lender** may require at any time for any purpose related to our credit transaction. I/we further authorize **Lender** to release such information to any entity it deems necessary for any purpose related to my/our credit transaction. I/we certify that the enclosed information (plus any attachments or exhibits) is valid and complete to the best of my/our knowledge. I/we authorize **Lender** to verify all my/our statements with any source, obtain credit and employment history, and exchange information with others about my/our credit and account experience.

NAME: (1)   SIGNATURE: (2)   DATE: (3)
ADDRESS: (4)   SOCIAL SECURITY #: (5)
CITY: (6)   STATE: (7)   ZIP: (8)   DATE OF BIRTH: (9)

NAME: SIGNATURE: DATE:
ADDRESS: SOCIAL SECURITY #:
CITY: STATE: ZIP: DATE OF BIRTH:

NAME: SIGNATURE: DATE:
ADDRESS: SOCIAL SECURITY #:
CITY: STATE: ZIP: DATE OF BIRTH:

NAME: SIGNATURE: DATE:
ADDRESS: SOCIAL SECURITY #:
CITY: STATE: ZIP: DATE OF BIRTH:

NAME: SIGNATURE: DATE:
ADDRESS: SOCIAL SECURITY #:
CITY: STATE: ZIP: DATE OF BIRTH:

5. <u>Social Security number</u>: Enter your complete Social Security number in XXX-XX-XXXX format.

6. <u>City</u>: Enter the city to match the address listed for #4.

7. <u>State</u>: Enter the state to match the address listed for #4.

8. <u>Zip</u>: Enter the zip code to match the address listed for #4.

9. <u>Date of birth</u>: Enter your date of birth in mm/dd/yyyy format.

CHAPTER 23

CLOSING: NEXT STEPS

A lot of material has been covered. In Part One, you learned about conventional and SBA business loans. You now know why I'm such a huge fan of the SBA loan programs. In Part Two, you learned about eligibility and all of the types of businesses and scenarios that qualify for SBA loan approval. In Part Three, you learned how to evaluate yourself, your partners, and your business so that you may put your best foot forward when applying for your business loan. In Part Four, you learned how to write an effective but streamlined business plan that gets the point across that your business will be successful and supports financial projections. In Part Five, you learned exactly how to complete each page of the application so that you will avoid the errors that cause so many delays.

So, you have done it! You are ready to apply for a business loan and especially an SBA business loan. For additional information and resources, visit www. ApprovedBook.com.

ABOUT THE AUTHOR

Phil Winn is a graduate of the University of Vermont, where he studied finance, management, and business law. In 2003 he joined a small commercial bank that specialized in SBA financing, and since then he has helped hundreds of entrepreneurs obtain over $100 million in business financing. He has had the privilege of training under some of the most highly regarded SBA leaders to fine-tune his expertise in the areas of SBA, traditional commercial lending and alternative financing.

Phil has always been passionate about entrepreneurship and helping others. In middle school, he formed a landscaping design and maintenance business employing several of his classmates. In high school, he began teaching skiing and snowboarding to people with disabilities and quickly became certified as a professional skiing instructor. Phil continued providing landscaping services and ski instruction through, and for a short period after, college.

Phil is the founder and CEO of Stanton Winn, a business loan advisory firm. Under the Stanton Winn umbrella, he leverages his interest in entrepreneurship, knowledge of finance, and his dedication to helping others by facilitating loan approval for entrepreneurs. He has developed streamlined processes for business loan qualification, business plan development, and navigating what can be a daunting approval process. To his clients' benefit, Phil enjoys studying loan credit policy and loan approval facilitation so that they need not do so. He wants his clients to focus on what they do best: running and growing their businesses. Phil specializes in traditional and alternative business financing, including commercial real estate, and is an advocate for the Small Business Administration's loan programs such as the SBA (7)a and SBA 504 programs.

For more about Phil Winn, visit www.PhilWinn.com.

Printed in the USA
CPSIA information can be obtained
at www.ICGtesting.com
JSHW022324140824
68134JS00019B/1290

9 781630 475635